Poole Bros.

Manual Third Presbyterian Church

Chicago, May 1, 1883

Poole Bros.

Manual Third Presbyterian Church
Chicago, May 1, 1883

ISBN/EAN: 9783337259686

Printed in Europe, USA, Canada, Australia, Japan

Cover: Foto ©Lupo / pixelio.de

More available books at **www.hansebooks.com**

MANUAL

THIRD PRESBYTERIAN CHURCH

CHICAGO,

MAY 1, 1883.

CHICAGO:
POOLE BROS., PRINTERS.
1883.

CONSTITUTION

OF THE

PRESBYTERIAN CHURCH.

The universal visible Church consists of all those persons, in every nation, together with their children, who make profession of the religion of Christ and submission to His law.

A particular Church consists of a number of professing Christians, with their offspring, associated for divine worship and godly living, agreeably to the Holy Scriptures, and submitting to a certain form of government. (*See* form of Gov., Chap. II.)

The Presbyterian Church, in the United States of America, was organized as at present in the year 1780, and the first General Assembly was held in the month of May of the following year. Its Constitution is embraced in the Westminster Confession of Faith and the Larger and Shorter Catechisms. The Doctrines of the Church are those formulated and maintained by the Reformers of the sixteenth century, in France, Holland, England and Scotland, and are essentially in harmony with the belief of all Evangelical Christians. While the Church holds to the excellence of its system of doctrine, it acknowledges that its most essential features are, the incarnation of the Son of God, His vicarious atonement, repentance, faith in our Lord Jesus Christ, and justification by faith alone, and this faith wrought by the Holy Spirit; and possessing this faith, the believer is entitled to the communion of saints.

In its outward organization, the Church is a unit; yet each particular congregation is free to move in its own sphere, as circumstances and local laws require, but conforming to the principles of the written Constitution.

As the Church session stands at the door of communion and membership, so the Presbytery is the judge of the qualifications of *its* members, and can admit, censure or depose, acting in the fear of God, and in accordance with His word.

The Synod is, in some sense, a larger Presbytery, reviewing the proceedings of the Presbyteries under its care, with power to redress whatever has been done contrary to order, to form new Presbyteries, and generally to take such action as shall tend to the edification of the Church.

The General Assembly is the highest judicatory of the Church. It decides all appeals and references brought from lower judicatories, reviews the proceedings of Synods, and gives advice and instruction to the whole Church in questions of law or morals submitted to it. It can decide all controversies respecting doctrine and discipline, and bear testimony against error in doctrine or immorality in practice in any Church, Presbytery or Synod. It may recommend changes in the Constitution, but a majority of the Presbyteries must approve before they are valid or obligatory.

Finally, the distinguishing features of the Church are, the equality of the clergy, as opposed to Prelacy or Episcopacy, and the equal voice of the laity in all ecclesiastical assemblies.

CHURCH OFFICERS.

(See form of Govt., Chaps. III. and IV.)

The ordinary and perpetual officers in the Church are Bishops or Pastors, the representatives of the people, usually styled Ruling Elders and Deacons.

The pastoral office is the first in the Church, both for dignity and usefulness. The person who fills this office hath in Scripture obtained different names expressive of his various duties. As he has the oversight of the flock of Christ, he is termed Bishop. As he feeds them with spiritual food, he is termed Pastor. As he serves Christ in His Church, he is termed Minister. As it is his duty to be grave and prudent, and an example to the flock, and to govern well in the House and Kingdom of Christ, he is termed Presbyter or Elder. As he is the messenger of God, he is termed the Angel of the Church. As he is to declare the will of God to sinners, and to beseech them to be reconciled to God through Christ, he is termed Ambassador. And as he dispenses the manifold grace of God and the ordinances instituted by Christ, he is termed Steward of the Mysteries of God.

RULING ELDERS.

Ruling Elders are the representatives of the people, chosen by them for the purpose of exercising government and discipline in conjunction with Pastors or Ministers.

This office has been understood, by a great part of the Protestant Reformed Churches, to be designated in the Holy Scriptures by the title of Governments, and of those who rule well, but do not labor, in word or doctrine. They not only have authority to receive members and exercise government and discipline in the Church, but are diligently to look whether every one properly deports himself; to admonish those who are disorderly, and to aid the Pastor in all things pertaining to the oversight and care of the flock. In case of a vacancy in the Pastoral office, they act under and with the advice of the Presbytery.

DEACONS.

(See form of Govt., Chaps. IX and X.)

The Scriptures clearly point out Deacons as distinct officers in the Church, whose business is to take care of the poor and to distribute among them the collections which may be raised for their use. To them also may be properly committed the management of the temporal affairs of the Church.

THIRD PRESBYTERIAN CHURCH.

The Third Presbyterian Church of Chicago was organized by a Committee of the Presbytery of Ottawa, consisting of Rev. Messrs. Patterson, Bascom, Wilcox, Walker and Henderson, on the 1st of July, 1847. At its organization, the church was composed of thirty-five members, of whom Messrs. Philo Carpenter, Henry Smith, Lawrens Kent and Gustavus W. Southworth were chosen Elders. The house of worship, a small frame building, situated on Union street between Washington and Randolph streets, was dedicated to the worship of God on the succeeding Sabbath, the 4th of July.

From the organization of the church until November, 1849, they enjoyed the ministerial labor of the Rev. J. B. Walker as their stated supply.

In November, 1849, a call was made out and presented to the Rev. Lewis H. DeLoss, of Rockford, to become the pastor of the church. In answer to this call, Mr. DeLoss commenced his labors in the church on the second Sabbath in November, 1849, and was duly installed as its pastor May 12th, 1850. On the 10th of June, 1851, the pastoral relations between him and the church were, by mutual consent, dissolved by the Presbytery.

On the 5th of October, 1851, Mr. Edwin G. Moore, a licentiate of the Presbytery of Franklin, Ohio, was invited to labor in the church, with a view to ultimate settlement as its pastor. Mr. Moore commenced his labors in the month of October, and was, on the 5th of November, 1852, called to settle with them as their pastor. Having accepted their call, Mr. Moore was ordained and installed over the church by a committee of the Presbytery on the 14th of the same month. The labors of Mr. Moore were continued until the autumn of 1854.

The Rev. Mr. Ferris, of the Dutch Reformed Church, supplied the pulpit from the succeeding spring until the call of Rev. Asahel L. Brooks to the pastorate of the church. Mr. Brooks was installed June 12th, 1856. This ministry was terminated, at his own request, November 17th, 1859.

On the 6th of February, 1860, the Rev. Arthur Swazey was invited to the pastoral care of the church. He began his labors on the 1st of April following, and was formally installed by the Presbytery September 12th of the same year.

Over five hundred persons were admitted to the church during the pastorate of Dr. Swazey, and a debt of some forty-five thousand dollars nearly extinguished. On the 16th of December, 1869, he tendered his resignation, which, at his earnest request, was accepted at a meeting of the church held the following day.

On the 13th of June, 1870, Rev. Abbott E. Kittredge, pastor of the Eleventh Presbyterian Church of New York, was elected pastor of this church, and on the 2d of October following began his labors, having been installed by the Presbytery on that day. Three churches have been organized during this period from our membership, the Reunion, Westminster and Campbell Park churches. Three Sabbath schools are under the care of this church, the Home school and the Foster and Noble Street Mission schools, with a total enrolled membership of 1,917 scholars.

In the autumn of 1877 the church edifice on the corner of Washington and Carpenter streets was sold to the congregation of the Reformed Episcopal Church, under the care of Rev. Bishop Fallows, and in May, 1878, the present edifice on Ashland avenue was occupied.

ARTICLES OF FAITH.

Article I. — We believe that there is one only living and true God — the Father, the Son, and the Holy Ghost — self-existent and infinite in every perfection, the Creator, Preserver and Governor of the Universe.

Art. II. — We believe that the Scriptures of the Old and New Testaments were written by holy men as they were moved by the Holy Ghost, and are the only infallible rule of faith and practice.

Art. III. — We believe that Jesus Christ, our Mediator, is truly God and truly man, and that, by his sufferings and death on the cross He made atonement for the sins of the world; so that the offers of salvation are sincerely made to *all* men, and all who repent and believe in Him will be justified and saved.

Art. IV. — We believe that those who are justified through faith in Christ are renewed by the Holy Ghost, according to the eternal purpose of God, and will owe their preservation in holiness and final salvation to grace alone and not to any works of righteousness which they have done.

Art. V. — We believe that the children of God are created in Jesus Christ unto good works, and that a renewed heart will evince itself in the various acts of an obedient and holy life.

Art. VI.— We believe that the sacraments of the New Testament are Baptism and the Lord's Supper; that Baptism is to be administered to none but believers and their households, and the Lord's Supper to be received by His disciples.

Art. VII.— We believe that Jesus Christ will appear at the end of time to judge the world; that the wicked will go away into everlasting punishment, but the righteous into life eternal.

FORM OF ADMISSION
TO
CHURCH MEMBERSHIP.

BELOVED FRIENDS : You have presented yourselves before God, and His people, and the world, to make a solemn confession of your religious faith, and to take upon you, in a public manner, the bonds of the everlasting covenant. We trust and believe that you have well considered the nature of this transaction, and have already offered yourselves a living sacrifice, holy and acceptable to God, through Jesus Christ. With regard to your doctrinal belief, we feel that, in this public act, but *one* doctrine is essential to your union with us, and vital to your spiritual health, and that is a hearty and intelligent belief in the Lord Jesus Christ, "God manifest in the flesh," and as such, your Almighty Saviour. In this one fundamental doctrine of our religion do you heartily believe?

[*Those who were not baptized in infancy will now be baptized.*]

You who were baptized in infancy do now reaffirm, for yourselves, the vows made in your behalf by believing parents at your baptism.

You will now enter into covenant with God and this church.

Believing it to be your duty to confess Christ before men, you do now, in the presence of God and this assembly, solemnly avouch the Lord Jehovah, the Father, the Son, and the Holy Ghost, to be your God and portion forever ; receiving the Lord Jesus Christ as your Prophet, Priest and King, and the Holy Ghost as your sanctifier, comforter and guide. You humbly and cheerfully devote yourselves to God, in the everlasting covenant of his grace; you consecrate all your powers and faculties to His service and glory; and, relying upon the promised aid of the Holy Spirit, you engage to walk in all the statutes and ordinances of the Lord; to assemble yourselves with His people for His worship; to keep holy the Sabbath day; to maintain family and secret prayer; and to honor your high and holy vocation by a life of piety toward God and benevolence toward your fellow men.

Do you thus covenant and engage?

Now, then, beloved in the Lord, let it be impressed on your minds that you have entered into the most solemn obligations, and that you have become sharers, also, in the promises of the Everlasting Father. See to it, that ye be not moved away from the hope of the Gospel.

[*Those who unite with the church by letter or certificate will rise and join with those who come on confession of faith, in entering into formal covenant with the church, the Pastor saying to them*]:

You, fellow-believers, do join yourselves to this church, and covenant to walk with its members in charity, faithfulness and sobriety; to submit to its government and the discipline which Christ has appointed, and strive earnestly for the peace, edification, and purity of the church. All this you promise and engage?

We, then, as a church, do affectionately receive you to our communion. We welcome you to this fellowship with us in the blessings of the Gospel, and promise to treat you with Christian affection; to watch over you with tenderness, and to offer our prayers to the Great Head of the Church to incline you to fulfil this solemn obligation.

The Lord bless you and keep you; the Lord make His face to shine upon you, and be gracious unto you; the Lord lift up his countenance upon you, and give you peace. "Now, unto Him that is able to keep you from falling, and to present you faultless before the presence of His glory, with exceeding joy; to the only wise God and our Saviour, be glory and majesty, dominion and power, both now and forever. Amen."

QUESTIONS FOR SELF-EXAMINATION.

The Pastor and Elders propose, for the spiritual improvement of each member of this church, the following questions:

1. Do you hate sin, and because it is in itself exceedingly sinful and odious?

2. Do you trust in Jesus Christ as your only Saviour from sin and death?

3. Do you love Christians, and do you delight in their society?

4. Do you make it a matter of conscience to attend the *weekly meetings* of the church?

5. Do you desire to know the Saviour in your domestic arrangements, in your place of business and in your social intercourse?

6. Are you watchful over yourself in every respect, especially over your tongue, in restraining it from evil speaking?

7. Do you pray in secret daily, morning and evening?

8. Are you at peace with all men?

9. Do you keep the Sabbath day holy, refraining from all words and deeds inconsistent with the sanctity of that holy day?

10. Are your *children* instructed in the truth, commended to God in prayer and educated for eternity?

11. Do you worship God in your family and acknowledge Him with thanksgiving at your meals?

12. Do you read your Bible daily and meditate on what you read?

13. What influence has religion on your habitual temper and conduct?

14. What are you doing for Christ and the souls of men?

15. What self-denial are you practising for Christ's sake?

16. Do you labor diligently to bring neglectors of public worship into the sanctuary?

17. Are you in the habit of praying and laboring for the salvation of individuals?

18. Is your religious influence felt in the family, in the church, and in the social circle?

IN THE MORNING ASK YOURSELF:

1. What good can I do to-day?
2. To what temptations shall I be peculiarly exposed?
3. In what particulars can I act more wisely than I did yesterday?

IN THE EVENING ASK YOURSELF:

1. What good have I done to-day?
2. What victory have I gained over temptation?
3. Have I been faithful in improving each moment for Christ?

OFFICERS.

PASTOR.
Rev. ABBOTT E. KITTREDGE, D.D.

ASSISTANT PASTOR.
Rev. W. S. POST, D.D.

ELDERS.

WM. OSBORN.
WM. L. LEE.
SAMUEL M. MOORE.
CHAS. L. CURRIER.
EDWARD M. TEALL.
DAVID BRADLEY.
JAS. A. HAIR.
FRANK E. SPOONER.
ALBERT G. BEEBE.

LOUIS F. BURRELL.
LOTHROP S. HODGES.
JOHN CRIGHTON.
THOS. KANE.
DEMING H. PRESTON.
CHAS. F. CHESSMAN.
JOHN S. CARPENTER.
THOS. GOODMAN, Treas.
R. N. TRIMINGHAM, Clerk.

DEACONS.

H. E. C. DANIELS, Treas.
A. H. KEESE, Sec.
W. D. MESSINGER.
JAS. S. HUBBARD.

WM. H. BRINTNALL.
HENRY A. OSBORN.
J. H. SNITZLER.
WM. H. BEEBE.

TRUSTEES.

DAVID BRADLEY, Pres.
ROBERT SCOTT.
FRANK E. SPOONER.
CHAS. L. CURRIER.

THOS. N. BOND.
JAS. A. HAIR.
LOTHROP S. HODGES.
SAM'L W. ADAMS.

JAMES P. KETCHAM, Treas.

USHERS.

JAS. A. HAIR.
JOSHUA EMERY.
A. B. CLARK.
HENRY A. OSBORN.
GEORGE MORGAN.

WM. A. GOODMAN.
JOHN WALLS SCOTT.
THOS. A. STRAYER.
A. W. BURKHARDT.
JOHN F. RICE.

MORGAN K. DEALE.

SEXTON.
PRATT HAMILTON.

REGULAR SERVICES.

Public Worship on Sabbath at 10.30 A. M. and 7.30 P. M.

YOUNG PEOPLE'S MEETING.

Monday evening at 8 o'clock.

Reading Room open from 7 to 8 and from 9 to 10.

LADIES' PRAYER MEETING.

Tuesday afternoon at 3 o'clock.

CONGREGATIONAL PRAYER MEETING.

Wednesday evening at 8 o'clock.

TEACHERS' BIBLE CLASS.

CONDUCTED BY THE PASTOR.

Saturday evening at 8 o'clock.

SACRAMENT OF THE LORD'S SUPPER

Is administered on the first Sundays in February, April, June, August, October and December.

There is also a New Year's Communion on the first Sabbath in January, at which time there is no reception of members.

INFANT BAPTISM.

On the Sabbath following each Communion season.

SUNDAY SCHOOLS.

HOME.

MEETS AT 2.30 P. M.

OFFICERS.

Edward M. Teall	Superintendent.
Chas. F. Chessman } Wm. A. Goodman }	Assistant Superintendents.
Henry W. Caldwell	Sup't of Infant Dept.
Louis A. Munson	Assistant Superintendent.
Mervin E. Johnston	Secretary and Treasurer.
A. W. Burkhardt	Ass't Sec. and Treas.
Chas. D. Mill	Librarian.
Seymour Morris	Ass't Librarian.

REPORT OF HOME SCHOOL FOR YEAR 1882.

Highest attendance any one Sunday	964
Lowest " " "	448
Average " " "	824
Scholars received into Church	58

Balance on hand last report	$ 79 07	
Total collections for the year	848 55	
		$927 62
Average collections for the year	17 31	

Donated Industrial School of our Church	$ 79 07
Amount collected for Young Ladies' Missionary Society	66 22
Donated Cook County Sunday School Association	25 00
" Women's Presbyterian Board for Miss Cummings	25 00
" toward building church in Willowdale, Neb.	50 00
" to W. B. Morton	25 00

THIRD PRESBYTERIAN CHURCH.

Donated Miss Hattie Powers, Missionary, Erzroum, Turkey	100	00
" First Presbyterian Church, Miles City, Montana (J. W. Strevell)	100	00
" Industrial School of our Church	100	00
" Rev. J. W. Snowden, Missionary American Sunday School Union, San Jose, Cal	50	00
" Rev. A. H. Campbell, Home Missionary, Casey, Iowa	50	00
" Presbyterian Church, La Dora, Iowa	100	00
" Presbyterian Church, near Fargo, Dakota (Mr. Morgan)	100	00
Balance on hand	57	33
	—$927	62

EDWARD M. TEALL, Superintendent.

FOSTER MISSION.

MASKELL HALL, 173 SOUTH DESPLAINES STREET.

MEETS AT 2.30 P. M.

OFFICERS.

CHARLES L. CURRIER	Superintendent.
RALPH N. TRIMINGHAM JAMES S. HUBBARD	Assistant Superintendents.
JAMES H. MILES	Treas. and Sec.
THOMAS KANE	Sup't of Infant Class.
WM. T. TEMPLETON	Asst. Sup't of Infant Class.
DAVID W. WOOD	Teacher of Bible Class.
H. N. NORTON	Librarian.

ABBREVIATED REPORT OF FOSTER MISSION.

Average attendance in 1882	407
Largest "	601
Smallest "	296
Number of teachers	45
Teachers and scholars united with church	5

TREASURER'S REPORT.

AMOUNT CONTRIBUTED BY THE SCHOOL.

January 1st, 1882.		
Balance on hand	$ 39	56
Sabbath collections (average $5)	261	43
Receipts for picnic	101	45
	$402	44

EXPENSES.

Papers, etc., for school	$185	59
Expenses of picnic	85	00
Sundry items	27	91
Christmas festival	82	15
Balance January 1st, 1883	21	79
	$402	44

In addition to the above amount, about $600 is appropriated from the Church Fund, making the total yearly expenses of the school $1,000.

The Infant Class numbers from 100 to 150 scholars, and the Bible Class from 25 to 40 members, while in connection with the same is held a weekly Prayer Meeting.

NOBLE STREET MISSION.

OFFICERS.

DANIEL FORDES	Superintendent.
W. H. BEEBE	Assistant Superintendent.
G. E. SHIPMAN, Jr.	Secretary and Treasurer.
H. J. SMITH	Librarian.
HEMMO HEIKEMA	Assistant Librarian.
MISS F. C. SHIPMAN	} Infant Department.
MISS M. C. SHIPMAN	

This school was taken under the care of the Third Church in January of this year, and the report, therefore, only covers the past four months.

Average attendance	300
Largest any one Sunday	352
Smallest " "	201
Teachers and officers	39
Contributions by the school since January 1st	$71 82

REPORT OF TREASURER OF THE SESSION.

RECEIPTS AND DISBURSEMENTS.

January 1st, 1882.

Balance in the Treasury.................................... $190 86
Receipts from January 1st, 1882, to May 1st, 1883, as follows, viz.:

COLLECTIONS.

For Sunday-school work................................$3,398	70	
" Foreign Missions...................................	1,337	33
" Home Missions.....................................	2,198	18
" Maywood Church...................................	250	00
" Redemption of Fallen Women.......................	157	53
" Ministerial Relief....................................	405	08
" Publication Society.................................	135	03
" Foundlings' Home.................................	74	77
" Education...	93	32
" Freedmen...	93	33
" General Fund.......................................	1,008	13

9,151 40

Total..................................... $9,342 26

DISBURSEMENTS AS FOLLOWS:

To Sunday-school work, including Home and Mission School......................................$3,217	44	
" Foreign Missions...................................	1,298	33
" Home Missions.....................................	2,198	18
" Maywood Church...................................	250	00
" The Society for Redemption of Fallen Women......	157	53
" Ministerial Relief...................................	405	08
" Publication Society.................................	135	03
" Foundlings' Home.................................	74	77
" Education Society.................................	93	32
" Freedmen's "	93	33
" Ladies' Benevolent Society.........................	378	00
" Church Manuals....................................	206	50
" Assessment of Presbytery..........................	157	95
" " " "	170	46
" Clothing for an aged minister......................	48	33
" Missionary boxes...................................	50	00
" Printing and stationery.............................	34	05
" Dr. Speer, for work among Chinese in Chicago......	25	00
" Hymns and leaflets.................................	38	25
" Communion plates.................................	9	60
" Church Register in hotels..........................	7	00
" Poor not otherwise provided.......................	29	00
" Sundry small items................................	16	41

9,093 56
Balance in Treasury, May 1st, 1883...................... 248 70

Total..................................... $9,342 26

THOMAS GOODMAN, Treasurer.

THE BOARD OF DEACONS.

The Deacons are organized as a Board with the Pastor as Moderator.

The Board hold regular meetings monthly, at which time the Treasurer gives a report of receipts and disbursements during the month. Reports from committees appointed to attend to cases of suffering are made, and new committees assigned to families whose names have been presented to the Board.

Report of the Treasurer of the Board of Deacons for the term commencing January 1st, 1882, and ending March 31st, 1883:

RECEIPTS.

Balance on hand January 1st, 1882	$157 06
Sacramental Collection for January, 1882	128 15
" " " February, 1882	119 56
" " " April, 1882	128 01
" " " June, 1882	112 79
" " " August, 1882	49 01
" " " October, 1882	145 87
" " " December, 1882	145 07
" " " January, 1883	127 47
" " " February, 1883	120 65
Thanksgiving Collection	44 92
Money refunded to the Board	71 40
	$1,349.96

DISBURSEMENTS.

For General Relief, January 1st, 1882, to March 31st, 1883	$611 00
Funeral expenses paid	15 40
Payments on Rose Hill Lot	360 00
Thanksgiving dinners for poor families	49 92
Bread and wine for Communion	49 90
Amount paid Treasurer of session	100 00
Miscellaneous expenses	4 75
Balance on hand March 31st, 1883	158 99
	$1,349 96

H. E. C. DANIELS, Treas.

CHICAGO, March 31st, 1883.

During the past twelve months aid has been extended to sixteen families and persons members of our Church. Of the above number one person has passed from the earthly communion to the heavenly.

One feature of the work of the Deacons the past year has been a regularly organized visitation of a large number of the congregation with a view to their becoming acquainted with each other.

The Deacons remembered our worthy poor on Thanksgiving and Christmas Days, providing all with good dinners.

The Board desire to ask the co-operation of the Church in their labors. They sincerely trust that persons who may at any time know of those in distress in our congregation, will promptly report their names to them that there may be no delay in rendering assistance.

The Deacons respectfully call the attention of the ladies of the church to the fact that frequent applications are made to them, not only for pecuniary assistance but for employment. They, therefore, request that whenever ladies have sewing or similar work suitable for women, they will, before applying elsewhere, ascertain whether parties can be furnished from the congregation to perform the same. Application can be made to any member of the Board of Deacons.

A. H. KEESE, Sec.

LADIES' BENEVOLENT WORK.

MRS. SAMUEL SHARP, PRESIDENT.

The Ladies' Benevolent Society has held eleven meetings for the season of 1882-3; one a call-meeting to complete unfinished work much needed at the time, and three all day meetings, at which lunches were served and a pleasant social time enjoyed. The largest number in attendance at any one time was 165 and the smallest 19. Forty-five dollars were received in membership fees, twenty of which were paid for our new sewing machine and the remainder went into the missionary box.

Two hundred and seventy-five dollars have been contributed by the session for the purchase of material, from which have been made 650 articles, including clothing, towels and bedding. There were also donated 75 second-hand garments, making in all 725.

Of the above 117 were sent to Park College, Mo.; 69 to Braidwood, and 11 articles were given to Miss Cummings, the medical missionary, while the balance, 528, were distributed here in the city. The following articles were also received by donation: nine yards Canton flannel from Mrs. Henry Osborn; one piece of goods and ten yards red flannel from Mrs. Schwartz; two calico dress patterns and three and a half yards muslin from Mrs. Little for the Braidwood sufferers.

The value of the above named articles, at a fair estimate, would be as follows: sewing machine, $20; one missionary box sent to Mr. Patch, $50; one box to Park College, Mo., $50; articles to Miss Cummings, $15. The 69 articles to Braidwood, together with the 528 distributed in the city, estimated at $400.

LADIES' PRAYER MEETING.

This meeting of the church was organized nine years ago, and has been sustained each week, up to the present time, without interruption.

The meetings are held every Tuesday afternoon in the church parlors. The third Tuesday of the month the subject of Foreign Missions is considered and the following week is devoted to temperance.

The influence of these meetings as a means of spiritual growth and strength to the church cannot be overestimated.

All the ladies of the church are cordially invited to attend these services, and by their presence and efforts increase the interest of the meetings and also promote their own spiritual welfare.

INDUSTRIAL SCHOOL.

MRS. A. G. BEEBE, PRESIDENT.

The Industrial School has held its sessions from 2 to 4 o'clock every Saturday afternoon, from November 18th, 1882, to April 21st, 1883, in the Holland Presbyterian Church, corner of Erie and Noble streets. The object has been to instruct girls in sewing, together with religious instruction, forty minutes being given to the latter at the opening of the school. Although the field of labor was a new one, the school opened with 148 scholars and 18 teachers and officers, and the interest in the work steadily increased until, on March 3d, there were present 227 scholars and 29 officers and teachers. The whole number of pupils enrolled has been 267, with an average attendance of 194. The whole number of teachers and officers enrolled was 44.

Average attendance 29. The number of garments finished by pupils, 311. Number of bed-quilts pieced, 79.

The school has been successful on account of the faithfulness and earnestness of the teachers, who have been unusually punctual in attendance and interested in the work.

Donations have been received from the Sunday School and Dr. Kittredge.

Bibles were awarded to pupils for perfectly committing the Scripture Catechism taught in the opening exercises.

WOMAN'S FOREIGN MISSIONARY SOCIETY.

MRS. C. N. HARTWELL, PRESIDENT.

This Society, organized twelve years ago, has since been engaged in active work without interruption, holding regular meetings the third Tuesday of each month, at 3 p. m., in the church parlors.

Its object is to disseminate missionary intelligence and to receive contributions for foreign missions.

The officers consist of a President, Vice-President, Secretary and Treasurer and Finance Committee. The Society numbers at present 246 members. The meetings are opened with prayer, singing and Bible reading, after which the monthly reports of Secretary and Treasurer are given; letters received from foreign fields are read, and items of interest connected with the foreign missionary work are contributed. The subjects for the meetings for the past year have been as heretofore, beginning with China for January, Mexico, India, Siam and Laos, Africa, North American Indians, South America, Japan, Persia, Papal Europe and the Syria mission. The support of two lady missionaries, Mrs. Kelso and Miss Olmstead, continues to be the special object for which the greater part of the fund received is appropriated.

Mrs. Kelso, of Lodiana, India, who a year ago visited America, has returned to her work in India, and recent intelligence received from her shows her increased zeal and interest in her life-work, with added health and strength following the rest so much needed. Miss Olmstead writes *beautiful* letters from Bankok, Siam, full of joy and consecration. She went forth three years ago to the work that God had chosen for her, and her efforts have been blessed in all she has been led to do.

Our own church has been honored: We have had the privilege of aiding in the preparation required in sending out one of our own number, a member of the Third Church, Miss Cummings, who goes as a medical missionary to Japan. Over three hundred dollars has been contributed through this Society toward her outfit.

Our pastor, Dr. Kittredge, has found time to come into our meetings on several occasions, and has given us words of encouragement and united his earnest prayers with ours in the cause which we represent.

Christian sisters, shall we not strive to do a grander work for Christ in the coming year, by sending the Word of Life to those who sit in darkness, that when the "Harvest Home" is sung and the laborers gather at sunset, we may come with our arms *filled* with sheaves saved for the granary of our Lord?

Treasurer's Report.

The total amount of money which has come into my hands as Treasurer of this Society, since the last annual meeting	$1,138	37
Balance in treasury from last year's account	38	77
Gift from Y. L. B. Society for Miss Olmstead's salary	100	00
Pledges paid after last annual meeting	9	50
Special gift for the Nestorians	10	00
Special fund	175	00
Pledges paid for the year closing to-day	805	10
Total	$1,138	37

Mrs. H. A. Osborn, Treasurer.

Expenditures.

This money has been expended as follows:

Envelopes and printing	$2 00
Expenses of missionary meeting in June	6 50
On account New England supper	12 00
Annual report	1 00
Members of Finance Committee for circulars, postage, etc.	12 80
For Nestorians	10 00
Mrs. Kelso's salary	400 00
Miss Olmstead's salary	450 00
	$894 30
In the treasury at meeting March 20th	244 07
	$1,138 37
Unpaid pledges	$134 85

Contributions to the Funds for Miss Cummings.

Seed Sowers	$10 00
Sunday School	25 00
Mrs. Story	1 00
Y. L. B. Society	25 00
Mrs. Hartwell	2 00
" Kane	35 00
" J. S. Knox	25 00
	$123 00

THE YOUNG LADIES' BENEVOLENT SOCIETY.

MRS. MARY O. LYMAN, PRESIDENT.

This Society, composed of the young ladies of the church, was organized January 17th, 1882.

During the first winter the young ladies appropriated $100 to Miss Olmstead in Siam, $57 to the Bible Readers' Home, and several smaller sums to various charitable purposes, and had, at their last meeting in May, 1882, $230.59 in the treasury.

During the fall of 1882 $100 was sent to Miss Olmstead, $25 to Miss Cummings and $13.89 to the Bible Readers' Home.

After January 1st, 1883, the young ladies gave a few mite socials, a Japanese tea party, and, after paying all expenses, had in the treasury $306.73, $300 of which was assigned to Mrs. Ash for the purpose of getting her in the Old Ladies' Home.

The Society adjourned May 6th, 1883, to meet again in September; with a balance in the treasury of $6.73.

IDA B. HAIR, Secretary.

THE YOUNG PEOPLE'S LIBRARY ASSOCIATION.

This Association was organized in October, 1880, and is composed exclusively of the young people of the congregation. In the words of its Constitution, "Its object is to develop the Christian character, improve the spiritual, intellectual and social condition of its members, and to inspire religious activity among all the young people of the church."

The growth and success of the Association has far exceeded the anticipations of its founders. It numbers now a membership of about four hundred, maintains an excellent free reading-room, and owns a circulating library of about one thousand volumes, which is held exclusively for the use of its members.

The work of the Association has been thoroughly systematized, and is divided among three general committees, as follows: A Devotional Committee, who have general supervision of the Young People's Prayer Meetings, select subjects, appoint leaders, and see that strangers visiting the meetings are cordially welcomed; a Library Committee, composed of five gentlemen having control of the Reading-Room and Library; and an Entertainment Committee, of eight ladies and eight gentlemen, having the management of the social gatherings and of all literary and musical entertainments.

As regards the general work of the Association, it may be said, briefly, that through its frequent socials it has brought the young people of the church together and bound them by ties of a common acquaintance and friendship. It offers them also the use of a circulating library in every respect equal to the best in the city. Spiritually its work is shown in largely increased attendance at the Young People's Prayer Meetings, now averaging an attendance of over three hundred, and in the very large number of its members, who have united with the church during last year.

While striving to supply to some extent the social and intellectual needs of our young people, it is beyond all else the desire of the managers that the Library Association shall be a growing power for good, and that its work and influence shall be seen and felt in the salvation of souls and the strengthening of our church.

TREASURER'S REPORT YOUNG PEOPLE'S LIBRARY ASSOCIATION.

RECEIPTS.

To Balance on hand at last Annual Meeting	$212 89
" Cash from membership	371 26
" " " complimentaries	6 00
" Entertainment by Prof. Cumnock and the Chickering Quartette	33 40
" Contribution Mr. J. K. Anderson	50 00
" " Mr. Thos. Kane	25 00
" Library Fines to May 1st (less incidental expenses)	33 68
	——$732 22

DISBURSEMENTS.

By Sociables	$145 60
" Library, purchase of books	219 50
" Subscriptions, magazines, etc.	102 26
" Sundries, catalogue and case	83 40
" Sundry expenses, postals, and printing	73 90
" Balance	107 56
	——$732 22

H. A. OSBORN, Treas.

THE SEED SOWERS.

MRS. W. W. FULLER, PRESIDENT.

The Mission Band of "Seed Sowers" was organized March 11th, 1882, and is composed of the little girls of the congregation, twelve years old and under. The meetings have been held every alternate Saturday, the time being occupied in sewing and religious and literary exercises.

The children have raised through their efforts during the year nearly $50, and will now assume the support of a child in some mission school. The meetings have been well attended and a growing interest manifested in the work by both parents and children.

CONDENSED STATEMENT

OF THE BENEVOLENCE OF THE CHURCH FOR THE YEAR.

Home Sunday School		$848 55
Foster Mission		362 88
Noble Street Mission		.71 82
Treasurer of Session		9,151 40
"	" Board of Deacons	1,192 90
"	" Ladies' Foreign Missionary Society	1,099 60
"	" Young People's Library Association	519 33
"	" Young Ladies' Benevolent Society	300 00
"	" Seed Sowers	48 00
To this may be added the receipts by the Board of Trustees		25,619 32
	Total	$39,213 80

MEMBERS RECEIVED

FROM JANUARY, 1882, TO APRIL, 1883.

On confession of Christ................................. 155
By letter from other churches........................... 182

Total for the year.................................. 337

Absentees... 73
Dismissed by letter..................................... 115
Total membership.. 2067

In Memoriam.

Mrs. Harriet A. Aiken..................................June, 1882.
Miss Hattie S. Besly........................December 31st, 1882.
Mrs. Mary Barr...July 22d, 1882.
John C. Coonley.......................................October 6th, 1882.
Miss Mary Dent.....................................February 26th, 1882.
Mrs. Minnie B. Dunwell................................April 30th, 1883.
Mrs. Sarah E. DeLoss...................................October 1st, 1882.
Mrs. Amanda DeChacon...................................February, 1882.
Fletcher Dennison......................................April 2d, 1882.
Mrs. Susannah Fitch..................................October 21st, 1882.
Miss Kate G. Innis..................................February 10th, 1882.
Miss Sarah E. Kerry...................................January 20th, 1882.
Mrs. Sarah C. Kelsey..................................April 15th, 1883.
Mrs. Georgiana O. Patterson...............................May 3d, 1882.
Joel Pettis...August 28th, 1882.
Mrs. Ann Russell....................................December 27th, 1882.
Mrs. Emily M. Rawson...................................March 30th 1882.
Mrs. Margaret R. Story.................................March 21st, 1882.
Charles Smart.......................................August 29th, 1882.
George H. Thomas......................................May 26th, 1882.
Mrs. Minerva Whitley....................................October, 1882.
Mrs. Rebecca D. Waller...............................March 21st 1883.
Henry G. Wormer......................................March 1st, 1882.

"These all died in faith."

"I would not have you to be ignorant, brethren, concerning them which are asleep, that ye sorrow not even as others which have no hope."

"They shall hunger no more, neither thirst any more, neither shall the sun light on them, nor any heat."

"And there shall be no night there; and they need no candle, neither light of the sun; for the Lord God giveth them light, and they shall reign forever and ever."

"Blessed are the dead who die in the Lord, for they rest from their labors, and their works do follow them."

> "One family we dwell in Him,
> One church, above, beneath:
> Though now divided by the stream,
> The narrow stream of death.
>
> "One army of the living God
> To His commands we bow;
> Part of the host have crossed the flood,
> And part are crossing now."

LIST OF MEMBERS.

Abdill, James C...............	1875	Allen, Miss Georgiana A.......	1876
Abram, Mrs. Ella E............	1873	Allen, Mrs. Jane..............	1876
Adams, Samuel W.............	1871	Allen, Thos...................	1877
Adams, Mrs. Fanny R..........	1866	Allen, Mrs. Eliza..............	1877
Adams, Mrs. Mary G...........	1873	Allen, Frank S................	1879
Adams, Chas. R...............	1876	Allen, Geo. R.................	1882
Adams, Miss Sophia B..........	1881	Allen, John M.................	1882
Adams, Miss Martha...........	1882	Altmyer, Fred'k T.............	1878
Adamson, Robt. J..............	1876	Alvord, Ira M.................	1877
Adamson, Mrs. Zuleika M......	1876	Alvord, Mrs. Emaretta.........	1877
Afleck, Wm....................	1881	Ames, Henry D................	1882
Afleck, Miss Mary.............	1881	Anderson, Wm. H.............	1865
Afleck, Miss Ellen.............	1881	Anderson, Mrs. Hannah Y......	1865
Agnew, John L................	1877	Anderson, David...............	1771
Agnew, Mrs. Nannie...........	1877	Anderson, Samuel P...........	1872
Aiken, James E.	1871	Anderson, Mrs. Sarah E........	1873
Aiken, Chas. R................	1876	Anderson, Miss Jennie E.......	1875
Ainsworth, Mrs. Mary..........	1876	Anderson, Mrs. Lillian M.......	1876
Aldrich, Mrs. Mae F............	1878	Anderson, Chas. E.............	1877
Alexander, Jas. G..............	1866	Anderson, Miss Belle...........	1879
Alexander, Geo. B.............	1872	Anderson, John G..............	1881
Alexander, Mrs. Elizabeth......	1872	Anderson, Mrs. Sarah E........	1881
Alexander, James..............	1882	Andress, Judson C.............	1871
Allen, Mrs. Eveline............	1857	Andrews, Miss Hattie..........	1877
Allen, Mrs. Anna C............	1871	Arkins, Mrs. Laura J...........	1877
Allen, Alexander S.............	1876	Armour, Mrs. Anne............	1876
Allen, Mrs. Eliza S.............	1876	Armstrong, Frank H...........	1874
Allen, Mrs. Charlotte A........	1876	Armstrong, Miss Lizzie A......	1878

THIRD PRESBYTERIAN CHURCH.

Arthur, James	1875	Barber, Mrs. Emma C	1877
Arthur, Mrs. Mary J	1874	Barker, Mrs. Sally May	1880
Arthur, Miss Annie E	1875	Barnes, Miss Ellen	1877
Ashley, Augustus G	1867	Barnes, Miss Charlotte	1877
Ashley, Mrs. Laura A	1867	Barnum, Mrs. Lucy F	1877
Ashley, Fred. S	1873	Barr, Wm. J	1875
Atchley, Edward B	1877	Barr, Mrs. Jane W	1879
Atchley, Mrs. Lucinda M	1877	Barrett, Mrs. Helen W	1879
Atwood, Geo. H	1880	Barrows, Chas. R	1875
Atwood, Mrs. Elvira A	1880	Barry, Miss Sophie J	1878
Austin, Mrs. Minnie	1871	Barstow, Miss Sophia E	1871
		Bartholomew, Mrs. Louisa	1873
		Bartlett, Mrs. Mary J	1877
		Bates, Mrs. Myra	1879
Babb, Miss Estelle J	1880	Baxter, Mrs. Fanny	1873
Babcock, Mrs. Maria W	1863	Baxter, Merwin W	1874
Babcock, Mrs. Ann	1874	Baxter, Andrew L	1877
Bacon, Mrs. Fannie	1881	Beard, Harry A	1874
Bacon, Robt. M	1881	Beatty, Wm. R	1880
Bacon, George	1883	Becker, Henry C	1878
Bache, Mrs. Carrie	1879	Becker, Miss Christina S	1878
Baird, Frank T	1871	Becker, Miss Helena	1878
Baker, George	1883	Becker, Miss Gertrude M	1878
Baker, Mrs. Mary M	1882	Becker, Miss Henrietta C	1879
Baker, Miss Laura	1882	Becker, Miss Annie D	1879
Baldwin, Mrs. Mary J	1868	Beckett, Mrs. Frankie J	1875
Baldwin, Miss Ella H	1878	Beebe, Wm. H	1872
Baldwin, Andrew S	1880	Beebe, Mrs. Kate K	1872
Baldwin, Mrs. Frances L	1881	Beebe, Albert G	1879
Baldwin, Mrs. Nettie A	1881	Beebe, Mrs. Francis L	1879
Baldwin, Miss Helen L	1881	Beebe, Leslie W	1880
Balfour, Jas	1877	Beecroft, Mrs. Lizzie	1872
Balfour, Mrs. Grace A	1877	Beek, Geo. N	1879
Balfour, Miss Grace D	1877	Beek, Mrs. Annie E	1879
Ball, Miss Frances	1880	Beek, Horace W	1879
Banks, Wm. H	1866	Beidler, Wm. H	1867
Banks, Mrs. Lottie	1866	Belding, J. M	1880
Banks, Miss Lulu	1881	Belfield, Henry H	1871
Barber, Wm. T	1877	Belfield, Mrs. Anne M	1871

Belfield, Wm. T	1881	Blascheck, Joseph	1879
Belfield, Chas. E	1872	Blascheck, Mrs. Mary A	1879
Bell, Miss Carrie M	1882	Blay, Miss Belle M	1882
Bennett, Rezin I	1880	Blodgett, Mrs. Martha	1883
Bennett, Mrs. Martha M	1880	Blood, Seth N	1877
Bent, Geo. P	1876	Blood, Mrs. Sarah J	1876
Bent, Mrs. Clara A	1876	Bochove, Henry R	1882
Benton, Wm. H	1877	Bond, Thos. N	1867
Besley, Mrs. Isabella	1872	Bond, Mrs. Sarah C	1867
Besley, Miss Corinne	1872	Bond, Wm. R	1878
Bews, Miss Mary L	1880	Bond, Mrs. Martha B	1878
Bigsby, R	1882	Bonnell, Mrs. Emily	1879
Bigsby, Mrs. Eliza	1882	Booth, Miss Sidney May	1880
Bigsby, Irving	1882	Booth, Spencer H	1880
Birdsall, Walter	1874	Booth, Mrs. Carrie L	1880
Birge, Manning D	1879	Borwell, Edward B	1880
Birge, Mrs. Maria S	1879	Borwell, Frank J. C	1880
Birge, Miss Mertice M	1879	Botham, Thos. H	1877
Birkhoff, Geo. Jr	1880	Bothwell, Miss Maggie	1881
Birkhoff, Mrs. Elizabeth	1880	Bowen, Mrs. Mary H	1876
Birt, Miss Emma	1882	Bowie, James W	1876
Bishop, Miss Maggie J	1881	Bradley, David	1871
Bishop, Miss Isabella	1882	Bradley, Mrs. Cynthia	1871
Black, Jas. P	1867	Bradley, Miss Mary	1882
Black, Miss Lizzie	1872	Bradshaw, Wm. D	1870
Black, Stanley P	1875	Bradshaw, Mrs. Mabel H	1879
Black, Mrs. Fannie	1877	Bradshaw, Mrs. Harriet P	1872
Black, Miss Mary R	1877	Brady, Miss M. Arabella	1875
Black, Mrs. Augusta	1881	Brady, Simon C	1877
Black, Miss Jennie M	1881	Bray, Miss Eliza M	1881
Blackford, Henry	1882	Bremner, Mrs. Helen J	1879
Blades, Mrs. Mary A	1878	Brennard, Mrs. Margaret A	1877
Blades, Miss Beulah J	1879	Briggs, Mrs. Anna R	1858
Blades, Miss Anna	1879	Briggs, Mrs. Elvira P	1873
Blades, Miss Lolo L	1882	Brine, Mrs. Anna M	1873
Blades, Miss Minnie F	1882	Brintnall, Wm. H	1871
Blair, Wm. T	1883	Brintnall, Mrs. E. Gertrude	1876
Blakeslee, Miss Mattie	1875	Britton, Albert M	1871
Blakesley, Fred. E	1881	Brockie, Miss Anna H	1882

THIRD PRESBYTERIAN CHURCH.

Brodie, James M 1871
Brodie, Mrs. Jane F 1871
Brokaw, Mrs. Mary J 1879
Brooks, Mrs. Elizabeth 1880
Brown, Miss Ella L 1874
Brown, Mrs. Helen J 1876
Brown, Miss Mary 1878
Brown, Mrs. Adelaide 1878
Brown, Warren F 1879
Brown, Miss Rachel 1879
Brown, Joseph 1882
Brown, Mrs. Maria 1882
Brownlee, Thos. H. R 1882
Brubaker, Miss Mary I 1881
Bruce, Mrs. Susan E 1882
Bruce, Robert 1882
Bruce, Mrs. Mary A 1882
Bruton, Mrs. Jennie S 1882
Bryant, Miss Emily J 1877
Bryson, Mrs. Julia 1857
Bryson, Miss Isabella J 1858
Bryson, John M 1872
Buck, Miss Millicent M 1881
Buchanan, Joseph 1882
Builder, John 1882
Bullwinkle, Benj. B 1876
Bullwinkle, Mrs. Angeline J .. 1876
Burdick, Frank H 1873
Burdick, Mrs. Olive E 1873
Burkhardt, H. S 1876
Burkhardt, Mrs. Bettie 1876
Burkhardt, M. L 1880
Burkhardt, Henry 1880
Burkhardt, Mrs. Elizabeth S .. 1880
Burkhardt, Miss Ella V 1880
Burkhardt, Albert A. W 1880
Burkhardt, Miss Alice C 1880
Burkhardt, George T 1880
Burkhardt, Miss Elizabeth 1880

Burkhardt, Miss Ella V 1882
Burns, Miss Emma J 1877
Burrage, Thomas B 1881
Burrell, Louis F 1871
Burrell, Mrs. Maggie A 1874
Burrell, John F 1879
Burt, Mrs. Harriet 1876
Burtis, William G 1879
Burtis, Mrs. Emma J 1879
Butler, Wm. A 1876
Butler, Mrs. Bessie 1876
Butler, Mrs. P. W 1877

Cady, Mrs. Laura 1880
Caldwell, Henry W 1882
Caldwell, Mrs. Hannah H 1882
Callen, Miss Margaret 1859
Callender, Frederick A 1877
Cameron, Mrs. Sarah T 1877
Campbell, William 1875
Campbell, William E 1875
Campbell, Mrs. Isabella 1875
Campbell, Miss Jeanie G 1875
Campbell, Miss Jessie E 1875
Campbell, Miss Mary E 1878
Campbell, Colin C 1882
Campbell, George W 1883
Cannon, Mrs. Ella M 1875
Capers, Mrs. Emma M 1875
Carlile, Miss Ella M 1878
Carman, Mrs. Sallie H 1877
Carman, Mrs. Hannah 1877
Carpenter, John S 1878
Carpenter, Mrs. Hattie A 1878
Carpenter, Miss Ida B 1878
Carrington, Mrs. Esther E ... 1874
Carroll, Mrs. Annie E 1870

THIRD PRESBYTERIAN CHURCH. 11

Carson, Francis.................. 1878
Carson, Oliver................... 1878
Cartland, Miss Bertie............ 1877
Cartland, Mrs. Priscilla W....... 1877
Cary, Miss Anna S................ 1877
Case, Francis W.................. 1880
Catlin, Wm. R.................... 1879
Cavener, Mrs. Ellen W............ 1875
Chadwick, Mrs. Annie............. 1872
Chambers, Miss Clara B........... 1871
Chandler, Frederick B............ 1877
Chandler, Mrs. Lydia DeK......... 1877
Chandler, William W.............. 1877
Chapman, Almon................... 1876
Chapman, Mrs. Elizabeth S........ 1878
Chapman, Mrs. Susan C............ 1882
Chappell, Mrs. C. H.............. 1882
Chappell, Charles Henry Jr....... 1883
Cherry, Chas. L.................. 1875
Cherry, Mrs. Minnie.............. 1875
Chester, Harry W................. 1881
Chessman, Chas. F................ 1872
Chessman, Mrs. Julia G........... 1872
Chessman, Chas. F. Jr............ 1877
Chessman, Miss Fannie............ 1880
Childs, Edward W................. 1881
Claghorn, James D................ 1882
Clapp, Mrs. Fannie............... 1876
Clark, Albert B.................. 1878
Clark, Mrs. Sarah H.............. 1878
Clark, Miss Lulu................. 1881
Clark, Benjamin T................ 1877
Clarke, Mrs. Harriet............. 1880
Clarke, Miss Mamie P............. 1880
Clarke, Miss Margaretta.......... 1880
Clark, Lemuel.................... 1873
Clarke, Mrs. Annie W. L.......... 1873
Clark, George W.................. 1875
Clark, Mrs. Cornelia............. 1875

Clark, Wm. G..................... 1875
Clark, Mrs. Lizzie............... 1875
Clark, Holly C................... 1876
Clark, Miss M. Carrie............ 1876
Clark, Miss Sarah L.............. 1882
Clarke, Charles T................ 1882
Clarke, Eugene H................. 1882
Clarke, Henry.................... 1882
Clark, Miss Hattie............... 1883
Cleland, Andrew M................ 1881
Cleveland, Mrs. Johannah......... 1883
Close, Mrs. Nettie E............. 1875
Clothier, Albert................. 1881
Clothier, Mrs. Minnie B.......... 1881
Coburn, Miss Emma................ 1875
Cochrane, Miss Inez M............ 1877
Cockfield, Henry................. 1878
Cockfield, Mrs. Henry............ 1878
Cockfield, Joseph................ 1878
Colburn, Mrs. Carrie H........... 1881
Cole, Mrs. Cornelia.............. 1868
Cole, Charles D.................. 1875
Cole, Mrs. Ella.................. 1875
Cole, John S..................... 1882
Coleman, George M................ 1873
Colston, Mrs. Margaret J......... 1877
Comfort, Mrs. Olive.............. 1873
Comfort, Miss Grace V............ 1879
Compton, Miss Elizabeth C........ 1876
Compton, Miss Minnie S. W........ 1878
Cone, Miss Roma B................ 1880
Cone, Mrs. Eliza................. 1876
Conrad, Irwin W.................. 1878
Conner, Miss Alicia.............. 1875
Conry, Dr. T. J.................. 1879
Conry, Mrs. C.................... 1879
Cook, Mrs. Catherine............. 1875
Coonley, Mrs. Lydia A............ 1875
Coonley, Miss Mary L............. 1883

THIRD PRESBYTERIAN CHURCH.

Corbett, John	1878	Currier, Mrs. E. Almena	1872
Corbett, Mrs. Mary A	1878	Currier, Charles L. Jr	1881
Corbett, Miss Ella J	1883	Currier, Orville P	1875
Corby, Edward L	1877	Curtiss, Miss Sarah E	1876
Cornell, Mrs. Henrietta W	1877		
Cornell, Miss Mary	1880		
Coulter, Henry C	1880		
Cowles, John T	1881		
Cowles, Mrs. Mattie E	1881	Dale, Jas. A	1874
Coxhead, Geo. C	1878	Dales, J. P	1879
Coxhead, Mrs	1875	Dales, Mrs. J. P	1879
Coxhead, Miss Harriet B	1875	Dally, Miss Anna R	1878
Crampton, Miss Carrie	1879	Damon, Mrs. Kittie	1880
Crane, Mrs. Mary	1858	Danforth, George C	1882
Crane, Chas. R	1878	Danforth, Mrs. Peachie W	1882
Crane, Miss Jennie A	1877	Daniels, H. E. C	1873
Crane, Miss Mary R	1877	Daniels, Mrs. Mary D	1873
Crane, Miss Katie	1877	Daniels, Franc B	1874
Crary, Oliver A	1866	Daniels, John H	1874
Cravens, Mrs. Nancy A	1882	Daniels, Mrs. Frances L	1874
Cravens, Miss Helen A	1882	Daniels, Mrs. Claudine	1879
Cravens, Miss Addie D	1882	Daniels, Taylor A	1880
Crawford, Jas. M	1880	Daniels, Mrs. Agnes	1880
Creswell, John	1866	Daniels, Wm. H	1882
Crighton, John	1876	Daniels, Mrs. Mary E	1882
Crighton, Mrs. Jessie	1876	Davidson, Jas. A	1875
Crighton, Miss Alice M	1876	Davis, Wm. O	1879
Crighton, Miss Jessie	1878	Davis, Elihu T	1880
Crooks, David L	1876	Davis, Mrs. Jennette K	1880
Crooks, Thomas	1874	Davis, Colby	1880
Crooks, Mrs. Anna	1874	Davis, Mrs. Effie	1880
Crooks, Miss Agnes	1876	Davis, Isaac	1882
Cross, Wm. A	1881	Davis, Mrs. Mary	1882
Cross, Leo. G	1881	Davis, John E	1883
Crozier, James	1882	Dawson, Josiah B	1877
Crozier, Mrs. James	1882	Dawson, Mrs. Ida B	1877
Culver, Fitz-Edward	1870	Dean, Miss Mary H	1876
Cummings, Miss Sarah K	1882	Dean, Miss Jennie	1881
Currier, Charles L	1870	Deale, Morgan K	1881

Deale, Mrs. Emily F	1882	Downs, Miss Augusta L	1871
Deale, Wm. G	1882	Downs, Miss Etta B	1871
Deale, Mrs. Clara H	1882	Downs, Walter B	1877
Decker, Henry	1880	Downs, J. Edward	1877
Decker, Mrs. Ann E	1880	Downs, Mrs. Mary A	1866
Decker, Benton C	1878	Downs, Miss Julia H	1878
Decker, Miss Cora E	1878	Downs, Miss Mary R	1878
Decker, Everett G	1881	Dox, Wm. H	1880
Decker, Miss Martha M	1881	Drake, Frank C	1881
De Groot, Miss Anna A	1881	Drent, Jacob R	1880
De Groot, Miss Lottie E	1881	Drent, Mrs. Rosa A	1880
Dehn, Julius J	1875	Drummond, Duncan	1874
Deming, Charles R	1882	Drummond, Mrs. Jane F	1874
Deming, Mrs. Eva M	1875	Drummond, Davis D	1882
Demples, Miss Susie	1881	Drummond, Robt. A	1882
Dempster, Mrs. Cecilia	1880	Drummond, Ralph A	1882
Dennison, Victor	1881	Drummond, Mrs. Agnes D	1882
Deuel, Alfred E	1877	Dubois, C. L	1875
Devers, Jas. H	1877	Dubois, Mrs. Kate	1875
Dew, Charles A	1880	Duerson, Mrs. Martha L	1878
Dewey, Washington	1876	Duff, John	1878
Dewey, Mrs. Zue	1876	Duff, Mrs. Agnes	1878
DeWolf, Mrs. Harriet L	1876	Duff, Miss Jennie A	1881
Dickinson, Miss Adelia M	1872	Duncan, Miss Lizzie A	1880
Dietrich, C. J	1880	Dunk, Miss Louisa	1881
Dietrich, Mrs. Hannah	1880	Dunk, Thomas H. W	1881
Dietrich, Miss Cora M	1880	Dunwell, Wm. C	1881
Dixon, Henry J	1874	Dutton, Walter V	1877
Dobie, John J. C	1881	Dutton, Mrs. Elizabeth E	1881
Dobie, Wm	1881		
Dobie, Mrs. Arabella	1881		
Dobie, Arthur L	1881		
Dobin, Mrs. Anna M	1878	Eager, Miss Ella A	1881
Dobin, Arthur	1877	Eager, Mrs. Annie M	1881
Dobin, John C	1880	Eager, Charles E	1883
Downs, Mrs. Lydia E	1851	Eastman, Mrs. Sarah C	1878
Downs, Myron D	1852	Eckel, Oliver W	1874
Downs, Miss Mary E	1866	Eckel, Mrs. Mary H	1874
Downs, Miss Clara G	1871	Eckel, Miss Nancy K	1875

THIRD PRESBYTERIAN CHURCH.

Edington, Mrs. Henrietta	1881	Fenn, Mrs. Elizabeth	1874
Edington, Miss Marietta	1881	Fenton, Alfred E	1875
Edington, Miss Augusta	1881	Fenton, Mrs. Eliza M	1875
Edwards, Ebenezer	1877	Ferrier, Miss Jane	1879
Edwards, Mrs. Mary	1877	Ferrier, Thomas	1872
Edwards, Miss Matilda E	1881	Ferrier, Mrs. Mary A	1875
Eger, Jacob	1878	Ferris, Geo. W	1871
Eger, Mrs. Lyda B	1879	Fewins, Miss Helena	1878
Elder, Samuel	1874	Field, Mrs. Sophia K	1881
Elder, Mrs. Kate E	1877	Fielding, Mrs. Ann	1860
Ellis, Mrs. Julia G	1866	Finch, Mrs. Margaret A	1878
Ellis, William	1879	Finch, Mrs. Charlotte C	1879
Ellis, Mrs. Grace	1882	Findall, Mrs. Hannah	1882
Elliott, Wm. S	1880	Fish, Henry	1871
Elliott, Mrs. Athaline	1880	Fish, Mrs. Seliner E	1871
Elliott, Miss Carrie L	1880	Fish, Miss Josephine L	1874
Elliott, Albert J	1883	Fishburn, Randolph E	1878
Eltzholtz, Miss Josephine	1880	Fishburn, Thomas F	1878
Emery, Joshua	1880	Fisher, Miss Ada J	1879
Emery, Mrs. Emily L	1869	Fisher, Orrin	1880
Emery, Miss Hattie P	1878	Fittz, Mrs. Eliza	1857
Enright, Miss Emma L	1880	Fitzsimmons, Mrs. Margaret	1878
Ervin, Hugh	1877	Flagg, Mrs. Ann J	1862
Ervin, Mrs. Henrietta	1877	Flagg, Miss Sarah	1863
Ervin, Miss Laura	1883	Fleming, Mrs. Isabella C	1876
Erwin, Miss Mary I	1880	Flinn, Miss Sarah T	1881
Evans, Miss Grace E	1880	Floyd, Miss Sarah	1876
Evenhuis, Miss Denie	1881	Fondell, John	1881
Evenhuis, Miss Jennie	1880	Fondell, Robt. T	1883
Everett, Mrs. Mary A	1881	Forbes, Daniel	1880
Eves, Miss Mary E	1877	Forbes, Mrs. Carrie G	1866
Ewing, Dr. George V	1882	Forman, Dr. John	1872
Ewing, Mrs. Elizabeth	1882	Forman, Mrs. Annie L	1872
Ewing, Alex. W	1883	Forman, Geo. L	1872
Ewing, Mrs. Annie I	1883	Forman, Miss Rose L	1874
		Forman, John Jr	1877
		Forman, Miss Annie	1877
Farr, Wm	1877	Forney, Henry C	1877
Fenn, John J	1874	Fort, Mrs. Mary A	1882

THIRD PRESBYTERIAN CHURCH. 45

Fort, Miss Helen M	1882		Gibson, Alured G	1880
Foster, Henry C	1871		Gibson, Mrs. Elizabeth	1880
Foster, Mrs. Anna M	1871		Gibson, Robt. W	1881
Fox, Mrs. Laura P	1874		Gibson, Geo. C	1881
Fraser, Mrs. Hattie E	1877		Gilbert, Miss Jennie M	1876
Fraser, Allan	1879		Gilbert, Geo. H	1877
Fraser, Mrs. Julia A	1879		Gilbert, Charles T	1877
Freeman, Harman C	1873		Gilbert, Mrs. Adelaide C	1877
French, Mrs. Martha	1874		Gilbert, William	1881
French, Charles B	1877		Ginther, Miss Augusta L	1877
French, Miss Minnie M	1880		Giordano, Joseph	1879
French, Mrs. Harriet A	1882		Giordana, Mrs. Virginia	1879
Fuller, Wm. W	1878		Giordano, Andrew	1881
Fuller, Mrs. Susan B	1878		Giordano, John	1881
Fuller, Miss Cornelia A	1879		Giroux, George	1877
Fuller, Henry H	1880		Giroux, Mrs. Libbie	1877
Fuller, Miss Bessie	1881		Glasner, Miss Ruth H	1880
			Glass, Miss Isabella	1875
			Glenn, Miss Harriet Hope	1874
			Goldsmith, Mrs. Louisa I	1871
			Good, Miss Carrie D	1881
			Good, Miss Lillian L	1881
Gale, Edmund E. W	1880		Goodman, Thomas	1871
Gale, Mrs. Melissa A	1880		Goodman, Mrs. Hannah J	1871
Galt, Mrs. Isabella A	1858		Goodman, Miss Annie M	1871
Gardner, Mrs. Susan	1877		Goodman, William A	1871
Garrott, Mrs. Florence L	1878		Goodman, Miss Laura L	1872
Gaskins, Thomas P	1880		Goodman, Mrs. Catharine	1878
Gaskins, Mrs. Effie E	1880		Goodman, Thomas C	1878
Gates, Miss Amanda E	1882		Goodman, Mrs. Jennie M	1879
Gates, Miss Marion B	1883		Goodman, John S	1879
Gayley, Malcom	1882		Goodman, Mrs. Mary C	1879
Gaynor, Henry	1877		Goodman, Miss Grace	1882
Gaynor, Miss Lucy A	1877		Goodwillie, Miss Carrie J	1877
George, Nelson H	1882		Gordon, William	1882
George, Mrs. Carrie K	1882		Gordon, Mrs. Cornelia A	1882
Gibson, Miss Minnie	1878		Gould, Webster	1874
Gibson, Miss Kate F	1878		Gould, Mrs. Clara P	1874
Gibson, Mrs. Frances	1880		Graham, Porter	1872

THIRD PRESBYTERIAN CHURCH.

Graham, Mrs. Mary A	1872	Haight, Mrs. Anna D	1882
Graham, Charles	1877	Haine, Miss Emma A	1879
Graham, Dr. David W	1877	Hair, Mrs. Eliza S	1868
Graham, Mrs. Ida A	1880	Hair, James A	1871
Graham, James	1879	Hair, Mrs. Amelia R	1871
Graham, Mrs. Mary P	1879	Hair, Miss Ida B	1878
Graham, Edward E	1882	Hair, Samuel G	1872
Graham, Mrs. Mattie A	1882	Hair, Mrs. Jennie L	1872
Graham, Miss Annie J	1882	Hair, Wm. F	1873
Gray, Miss Lizzie	1882	Hair, Samuel F	1874
Graves, Dwight W	1871	Hair, B. M	1882
Greenwood, Mrs. Susan H	1877	Hair, Mrs. Hattie R	1882
Green, Mrs. Sarah E	1878	Hale, Mrs. Ellen Isabella	1863
Gridley, Charles C	1880	Hale, Miss Lizzie M	1875
Grinnell, G. G	1874	Hale, Miss Mary B	1877
Grinnell, Mrs. Catharine	1874	Hale, Otis H	1877
Grinnell, Miss Grace A	1877	Hales, Mrs. B. F	1881
Grinnell, Miss Florence I	1877	Hall, Mrs. Flora B	1872
Griffith, Thomas S	1879	Hall, Lemuel R	1873
Gritzner, Fred. A	1879	Hall, Mrs. Augusta A	1867
Gritzner, Miss Mary A	1880	Hall, Wm. A	1877
Gritzner, Mrs. Adelia	1880	Hall, Miss Edith B	1881
Grubb, Geo. G	1875	Hall, Miss Alfarata R	1881
Grubb, Mrs. Juliette	1875	Hall, Miss Belle	1882
Guffin, Mrs. Harriet N	1879	Hall, Miss Elizabeth	1882
Guilford, Alvin J	1881	Hall, Mrs. Rachel R	1882
Gunderson, Miss Hilda S	1877	Hallett, Mrs. Olive	1876
Gunderson, Wm. P	1883	Hamilton, Pratt	1877
Gunn, Mrs. Catherine	1875	Hamilton, Mrs. Susan V	1877
Gunn, Miss Jessie	1875	Hamilton, Paul H	1879
Gurrad, Miss Clara L	1876	Hamlin, Frederick N	1877
Guy, Mrs. Lucella B	1875	Hamlin, Mrs. Nettie M	1877
Gwathmey, Mrs. Elizabeth	1872	Hamlin, Everlin B	1873
		Hamlin, Mrs. Helen D. W	1873
		Hammond, Miss Hannah	1880
		Hand, Bayard E	1880
Hagan, Mrs. Mary	1872	Hand, Mrs. Anna B	1880
Haigh, Mrs. Eva L	1882	Hanley, Miss Isabel M	1883
Haight, Edgar A	1881	Hanning, Jas. T	1881

THIRD PRESBYTERIAN CHURCH. 47

Hannis, Mrs.	1877		Heath, Mrs. Ellen	1878
Hardy, Mrs. Jane W.	1876		Heath, Jas. M.	1881
Hardy, Fanny W.	1877		Heckler, Harry A.	1876
Hardy, Wm. M.	1877		Heegaard, Miss Petrea M.	1874
Hardy, Miss Alice J.	1881		Heermans, Miss Anna A.	1877
Harris, Charles	1872		Heermans, Paul W.	1883
Harris, Wm.	1882		Heffling, Addison B.	1880
Hart, Miss Elenora F.	1881		Heffling, Mrs. Mary M.	1880
Hart, Joseph C.	1882		Helm, Henry T.	1883
Hartwell, Mrs. Caroline N.	1873		Helm, Mrs. Julia F. L.	1883
Hartwell, Miss Nellie L.	1882		Helm, Scott	1880
Hartzell, Elmer	1876		Helm, Miss Nellie	1883
Hartzell, Miss Mattie	1877		Helm, Miss Alice	1883
Haskell, Mrs. Ellen R.	1874		Helm, Miss Judith	1883
Haskins, Mrs. Helen M.	1882		Henderson, Andrew M.	1882
Hatch, Mrs. Celia P.	1876		Henderson, Mrs. Agnes L.	1882
Havens, Mrs. Louisa A.	1882		Henderson, Miss Carrie B.	1882
Havens, Miss Carrie B.	1882		Hendrie, Chas. C.	1876
Havens, Miss Louisa M.	1882		Hendrie, Miss Mary E.	1879
Havens, Miss Fannie W.	1882		Henkel, Miss Emma F.	1880
Haverkampf, John L.	1882		Hensler, Mrs. Julia A.	1879
Haverkampf, Mrs. Mary	1882		Herbert, Edmund	1874
Haverkampf, Miss Anna	1882		Herbert, Mrs. Mary	1874
Hawes, Mrs. Jennie	1881		Hertig, Miss Elmira	1882
Hawkins, Miss Alice	1879		Hesse Henry	1883
Hawkins, Mrs. Salina	1878		Hesse, Mrs. Agnes	1883
Hawkins, Mrs. Selina C.	1879		Hewett, Austin C.	1879
Hawkins, Miss Etta V.	1881		Hewett, Mrs. Martha B.	1879
Hawkinson, Miss Amanda M.	1876		Hickcox, Benj.	1882
Hawkinson, Miss Nellie P.	1876		Hickcox, Mrs. Helen M.	1882
Haycock, Mrs. Anna M.	1880		Higgie, Miss Mary L.	1883
Hayes, Wm. H.	1876		Hill, Mrs. Esma	1872
Hayes, Mrs. Elizabeth M.	1876		Hill, John	1876
Hazen, Mrs. Sarah A.	1877		Hill, Mrs. Elizabeth	1876
Hazeltine, Miss Rebecca E.	1866		Hill, Miss Hattie H.	1880
Heaton, Wm. L.	1873		Hill, Edgar P.	1880
Heaton, Mrs. Bessie D.	1874		Hill, H. H.	1880
Heaton, Mrs. Margaret J.	1877		Hill, Mrs. S. E.	1880
Heath, John H.	1878		Hill, Mrs. Sarah E.	1891

Hiltabidel, Mrs. Annie 1879
Hiltabidel, Miss Lulu 1879
Hinchman, Miss Emma M 1881
Hitchcock, Chas 1874
Hitchcock, Miss Ella L 1879
Hobbs, Henry H 1877
Hobbs, Mrs. Kate R 1877
Hobbs, John D 1878
Hobbs, Miss Alma M 1880
Hobbs, Mrs. Mary C 1880
Hockaday, Miss Mary 1878
Hodges, Lothrop S 1872
Hodges, Mrs. Helen 1872
Hoelzer, Geo. W 1878
Hoffmann, Miss Carrie B 1871
Hoffman, Mrs. Carrie M 1876
Hoffman, Geo. D 1877
Hoffman, Luis 1880
Hofman, Miss Susanna F 1879
Hofman, Miss Henrietta J 1879
Hofman, Miss Cornelia M. H ... 1882
Holden, Mrs. Isabella 1865
Holden, Mrs. Louise R 1877
Hollingsworth, Achilles 1877
Hollister, Frank P 1873
Holmes, David H 1880
Holmes, Mrs. Rebecca 1880
Holmes, James C 1882
Holmes, Mrs. Mary E 1882
Holmes, Miss Mary L 1882
Holmes, Mrs. Mary B 1883
Holtzlander, Mrs. Sarah 1881
Hood, John W 1881
Hood, Mrs. Mary Alice 1881
Horn, Geo. E 1881
Hosking, Benjamin T 1882
Hosking, Mrs. Carrie J 1882
Hoskins, Benjamin 1872
Hoskins, Mrs. Sarah T 1881

Houston, Edward C 1877
Houston, Mrs. Ann 1877
Houston, John T 1879
Hovell, Miss Mary F 1882
Howard, Mrs. E 1877
Howe, Mrs. Laura J 1882
Howell, Mrs. Eva W. H 1870
Hoysraadt, Miss Blanche 1881
Hoyt, Dr. A. W 1880
Hubbard, Jas. S 1872
Hubbard, Mrs. Anna E 1872
Hubbell, Miss Hattie 1882
Hudson, James 1878
Hudson, Mrs. Sarah A 1878
Hughes, Hugh 1874
Hughes, Mrs. Laura D 1874
Hughes, Miss Sarah 1875
Hughes, Miss Elizabeth 1875
Hughes, Mrs. Mary A 1878
Hughes, Miss Adele 1880
Humberstone, Mrs. Carrie A 1874
Humphrey, Mrs. Harriet 1882
Humphreys, Alfred O 1881
Hunt, Wm. H 1857
Hunt, Mrs. Martha 1860
Hunt, Mrs. Jennie 1877
Hunt, Mrs. J. O 1882
Hunter, Thos. J 1878
Hunter, Mrs. Margaret S 1878
Hunter, John L 1883
Hurd, Darwin M 1866
Hurd, Frank W 1866
Hurd, Miss Julia E 1866
Hurdle, John G 1877
Hurdle, Armstead L 1881
Hussander, Geo. H 1876
Hussander, J. E 1876
Hutchinson, Mrs. Meda 1880
Hutchinson, Miss Eva A 1880

Hyers, Geo. A	1876	Jones, Mrs. Elizabeth	1872
Hyers, Mrs. Frances	1876	Jones, Thomas	1874
Hypes, Wm. T	1880	Jones, David L	1874
		Jones, Arthur B	1875
		Jones, Miss Esther E	1875
		Jones, Miss Annie	1878
Ingold, Arthur J	1881	Jones, Miss Rose F	1879
Innis, Hugh	1876	Jones, Mrs. Eliza A	1880
Innis, Mrs. Hugh	1879	Jones, Miss Marion L	1881
Inness, Hugh	1877	Jones, Mrs. Almira P	1881
Irwine, George	1882	Jones, Mrs. Elizabeth	1883
		Jordan, Miss Georgiana S	1874
		Jordan, Joseph D	1874
		Joss, Sewell E	1880
Jacobson, Miss Sophie	1879	Judd, Miss Emily P	1873
Jacoby, Mrs. Kate	1881		
Jameson, Gavin	1877		
Jameson, Mrs. Effie B	1877		
Jenkins, Miss Laura B	1876	Kane, Thos	1876
Jennings, Pearson D	1875	Kane, Mrs. A. E	1876
Jewell, Oliver P	1872	Kant, Chas	1882
Jilson, Mrs. Jane	1874	Keese, A. Hoffman	1872
Johnson, Mrs. Martha L	1868	Keese, Mrs. Elizabeth F	1864
Johnson, Miss Lizzie	1875	Keese, Mrs. Cornelia H	1872
Johnson, Royal F	1875	Kellberg, Adolph Emil	1879
Johnson, Louis G	1877	Kelly, Wm: A	1879
Johnson, Miss Daisy M	1878	Kellogg, Mrs. A. F	1882
Johnson, Edgar M	1880	Kellogg, Othniel W	1883
Johnson, Mrs. Harriet S	1880	Kelsey, Miss Sarah P	1871
Johnson, Albert L	1882	Kelsey, Miss Alice S	1881
Johnston, Mrs. Judith C	1871	Kemper, Mrs. Mary A	1883
Johnston, Mrs. Dora	1871	Kempster, Sam'l W	1879
Johnston, Mervin E	1876	Kempster, Miss Fannie E	1881
Johnston, Sidney B	1878	Kempster, Alfred E	1882
Johnston, Mrs. Louisa M	1878	Kemsley, Mrs. Annie	1879
Johnston, Miss Fanny F	1879	Kennedy, Miss Mary	1881
Johnston, H. Morris	1881	Ker, Chas. H	1879
Johnston, Mrs. Mary L	1881	Ker, Chas. H. Jr	1879
Jolly, Mrs. Isabella S	1876	Ker, Mrs. Sarah V	1879

Kerr, A. Newton	1875	Konkel, Chas. W	1882
Kerr, Miss Rebecca	1879	Kraybill, Eli W	1875
Kerr, Mrs. Kate	1881	Kraybill, Mrs. Lizzie E	1875
Ketcham, Jas. P	1877	Kraybill, Miss Anna G	1881
Ketcham, Mrs. Agnes C	1873	Krigger, Miss Lilly F	1874
Ketcham, Frank D	1877		
Killen, Henry S	1881		
Killen, Jonathan E	1882		
Killen George E	1883	Lake, Frank D	1878
King, Miss Eliza K	1879	Lamb, Mrs. Anna	1866
King, Chas. H	1881	Lamb, Mrs. Argent E	1872
King, Mrs. Ella M	1880	Landis, Thos. I. S	1881
Kirkham, Miss Louise A	1879	Landis, Chas. L	1883
Kirkham, Geo	1879	Lane, Joseph	1859
Kirkpatrick, Mrs. C	1877	Lane, Mrs. Helen D	1866
Kirkwood, Miss Elizabeth M	1876	Lane, Julius A	1872
Kittredge, Miss Emma A	1878	Lane, Miss E. F	1881
Kittredge, Miss Mabel H	1878	Lane, Mrs. Sophia L	1882
Kline, Daniel H	1877	Langlotz, Karl A	1879
Kline, Mrs. Althea W	1877	Lanterman, Perry M	1874
Klingenberger, A	1877	Larrabee, Mrs. Julia S	1869
Knight, Miss Julia H	1877	Lathrop, Mrs. Frances	1875
Knight, T. D	1878	Lathrop, Mrs. Ann S	1879
Knight, Mrs. Martha T	1878	Laughton, George	1873
Knight, Miss Kitty M	1878	Lavis, Wm. H	1879
Knight, Thos. A	1877	Lavis, Mrs. Jane E	1879
Knott, Frank P	1879	Lavis, Mrs. Anna	1879
Knowlton, Mrs. Austria C	1879	Law, Mrs. Eliza J	1872
Knowlton, Miss Hattie G	1882	Lawrence, Wm. E	1879
Knowlton, Mark D	1882	Lawrence, Mrs. Clara	1879
Knowlton, Mrs. Abbie E	1882	Ledgerwood, Robert E	1878
Knowlton, Miss Grace E	1882	Lee, Wm. L	1866
Knowlton, Miss Annie D	1882	Lee, Mrs. Deborah	1866
Knox, Dr. J. S	1873	Lee, Mary	1871
Knox, Mrs. Elizabeth H	1873	Lee, John W	1873
Knox, Geo. G	1876	Leeper, Wm	1876
Knox, Mrs. Elvira J	1873	Lettellier, Mrs. Eliza F	1876
Knox, Mrs. Susan	1878	Lewis, Theodore P	1870
Knox, Miss Mary E	1878	Lewis, Mrs. Louisa J	1870

THIRD PRESBYTERIAN CHURCH. 51

Little, Mrs. Mary S............. 1868
Little, Isaac................... 1877
Little, Mrs. Louisa............. 1877
Little, S. Miller............... 1879
Littlejohn, George.............. 1882
Lloyd, Miss Emma................ 1864
Lloyd, Miss Eugenie............. 1874
Lloyd, Mrs. Sarah J............. 1875
Lloyd, James.................... 1877
Lloyd, Mrs. Eliza............... 1879
Lobdell, Miss Rovilla........... 1872
Loder, Miss Anna B.............. 1874
Loder, Miss Rebecca E........... 1878
Loder, Mrs. Hannah.............. 1878
Logan, Miss Susan J............. 1876
Lord, Edward P.................. 1858
Loury, Alex..................... 1878
Lowry, Mrs. Martha B............ 1880
Ludlow, George M................ 1883
Ludlow, Andrew W................ 1883
Lyman, Mrs. Mary A.............. 1876

Macauley, Miss Emma M........... 1878
Macdonald, John F. W............ 1880
Mackey, Æneas S................. 1883
Mackin, Jas. H.................. 1880
Mallinson, John R............... 1882
Mallory, Frank.................. 1878
Marrillar, Mrs. Mary............ 1876
Marsh, Mrs. Carrie H............ 1877
Martin, Miss Eunice A........... 1874
Martin, George.................. 1876
Mason, Mrs. J. R................ 1872
Mason, Nelson................... 1874
Mason, Mrs. Desire.............. 1874
Mason, Geo. A................... 1881
Mason, Mrs. Mary E.............. 1882

Mather, John H.................. 1872
Mather, P. L.................... 1877
Matteson, William............... 1872
Matteson, Mrs. Isabella......... 1872
Mathews, Mrs. Margaret.......... 1878
Mathews, Miss Grace I........... 1877
Mathews, Chas. Hale............. 1875
Matthews, Mrs. Mary F........... 1871
Maxsee, Mrs. Abbie O............ 1873
Maxwell, W. R................... 1882
May, Gustave A. Jr.............. 1877
Maybee, Charles................. 1875
McAdam, Mrs. Agnes.............. 1878
McAllister, Jas. M.............. 1881
McAllister, Mrs. Hattie L....... 1881
McAllister, Mrs. Jeanette....... 1883
McArthur, Mrs. J................ 1874
McArthur, Miss Ada J............ 1875
McArthur, Mrs Mary A............ 1880
McArthur, Mrs. Harriet.......... 1880
McCabe, Chas. R................. 1880
McCammon, Miss Sarah J.......... 1882
McCammon, Miss Annie............ 1882
McChesney, Miss Maggie S........ 1883
McClelland, Thomas H............ 1882
M'Clory, William................ 1878
M'Clory, Fred. S................ 1878
M'Clory, Henry.................. 1883
M'Clory, Mrs. Matilda........... 1883
M'Clory, Clement................ 1883
McClure, Mrs. Hannah............ 1874
McClure, Lester J............... 1882
McCormick, Mrs. Fannie E........ 1881
McCrea, Miss Katie.............. 1874
McCulloch, Miss Elizabeth....... 1860
McCullough, Dr. J. R............ 1873
McCullough, Mrs. J. R........... 1873
McDermid, Donald................ 1877
McDermid, Mrs. D................ 1877

McDonald, Miss Jennie 1875	Meacham, Mrs. Hattie E 1881
McDonald, Mrs. Abbie A 1878	Means, George R 1880
McDougall, Daniel 1873	Means, Mrs. Sarah I 1880
McDowell, Thomas 1873	Medill, Mrs. H. B 1870
McDowell, Mrs. Mary E 1875	Melcher, Charles 1876
McEldowney, Stewart B 1878	Melcher, Mrs. Charles 1876
McEldowney, Mrs. Lizzie 1878	Melcher, Wm. G 1877
McGillivray, Edward W 1882	Mendsen, William 1871
McGowan, Frank 1872	Mendsen, Mrs. Julia 1871
McGowan, Mrs. Susan F 1872	Merchant, John A 1882
McGowan, Mrs. Lily H 1878	Merrimee, Mrs. Jennie 1878
McGregor, Douglas J 1872	Merriman, Mrs. Josephine J 1864
McHaiton, Samuel G 1882	Merriman, Miss Ida L 1877
McKay, Mrs. Margaret 1872	Merriman, Chas. J 1879
McKee, Miss Ellen 1882	Merriman, Miss Emily S 1880
McKinney, George 1883	Merriman, Miss Mable S 1882
McKinney, Mrs. Elizabeth J 1883	Merrit, Mrs. Elizabeth S 1879
McKnight, Mrs. Lizzie 1874	Merritt, Mrs. Ellen L 1882
McKnight, Miss Nellie B 1882	Messinger, Wm. D 1867
McLaren, Peter 1876	Messenger, Mrs. Ella J 1873
McLaren, Mrs. Martha J 1876	Meuser, Bernard 1882
McLaren, Miss Maggie 1880	Michaels, Miss Jennie D 1871
McLaren, Miss Clarrissa 1880	Michaels, Chas. D 1873
McLean, Robert C 1876	Michaels, J. C 1875
McLean, Mrs. Ellen M 1880	Michaels, Miss Fannie D 1875
McLean, Dr. John 1882	Mickens, Jeremiah R 1878
McLean, Mrs. Jane L 1882	Miles, Jas. H 1873
McLean, John D 1875	Miles, Mrs. Sarah A 1864
McLean, Miss Gaetana 1880	Miles, Miss Clara Belle 1874
McLelland, Dr. Alex. S 1878	Miles, Miss Hattie P 1880
McLelland, Mrs. Catherine A ... 1878	Mill, Jas. W 1860
McLenahan, M. B 1872	Mill, Chas. D 1873
McLenahan, Miss Minnie 1872	Miller, Miss Hattie 1872
McLeod, Miss Sarah 1869	Miller, Miss Carlotta L 1875
McLeod, Mrs. Isabella 1872	Miller, Henry W 1881
McMasters, Mrs. Annie E 1878	Miller, Mrs. Ellen 1881
McMurphy, Mrs. Malvina 1881	Miller, Miss Barbara 1881
McNeal, Miss Margaret 1875	Miller, Miss Alice 1882
Meacham, Dudley A 1881	Mills, Dr. Jas. P 1870

THIRD PRESBYTERIAN CHURCH.

Mills, Mrs. Anna M	1879	Morgan, Wm. B	1871
Mills, John N	1879	Morgan, Mrs. Agnes S	1871
Mills, Cecil	1880	Morgan, William	1871
Miner, Henderson H	1880	Morgan, Henry J	1871
Miner, Miss Minnie M	1881	Morgan, Mrs. Abbie G	1871
Ming, Moy Luke	1882	Morgan, Miss Fannie L	1873
Minich, Mrs. Emma F	1872	Morgan, Mrs. Mary J	1876
Mitchell, Mrs. Catharine A	1874	Morgan, Seward D	1876
Mitchell, Hugh	1875	Morgan, George	1876
Mitchell, Mrs. Nellie A	1875	Morgan, Mrs. Julia E	1876
Mitchell, William	1877	Morgan, Arthur M	1881
Mitchell, Mrs. Mary	1882	Morgan, Geo. C. Jr	1881
Mitchell, Miss Elsie E	1882	Morgan, Miss Sadie	1881
Molinelli, Miss Deva	1880	Morgan, Homer B	1882
Molinelli, Mrs. Catherine	1880	Morgan, Henry H	1882
Molinelli, Andrew	1880	Morlan, Chas. M	1881
Molinelli, Mrs. Mariana	1880	Morrison, J. C	1877
Monaghan, Mrs. Stella E	1879	Morse, Chas. H	1875
Money, John M	1878	Morse, Mrs. Laura C	1875
Money, Mrs. Sarah A	1878	Morse, Miss Evangeline	1877
Money, Wm. H	1882	Morse, Miss Ida	1879
Montgomery, Miss Elizabeth	1876	Morse, Miss Lilian	1881
Montgomery, Miss Louisa	1876	Morton, Mrs. Agnes C	1878
Montgomery, B. C	1878	Moulton, Rollin H	1876
Montgomery, Mrs. Sarah A	1878	Moulton, Mrs. Julia A	1876
Moore, Samuel M	1872	Moulton, Arnold Richard	1883
Moore, Mrs. Martha	1872	Muir, David	1874
Moore, French	1872	Muir, Mrs. Margaret	1874
Moore, Miss Samuella	1872	Muir, Miss Maggie	1875
Moore, Miss Rosina B	1872	Muir, William	1875
Moore, Miss Nona	1873	Muir, Jas. S	1875
Moore, Fred. E	1881	Mulick, Mrs. Sarah	1878
Moore, Mrs. Anna W	1881	Mullen, Mrs. Eliza	1876
Moorehouse, Mrs. Mattie	1880	Munson, Louis L	1878
Morgan, Henry M	1860	Murray, Alexander	1870
Morgan, Mrs. Mary Ella	1863	Murray, Mrs. Isabella	1870
Morgan, Miss Catherine	1866	Murray, Magdalen	1870
Morgan, Miss Harriet	1866	Murray, Albert D	1871
Morgan, Mrs. Catharine	1866	Murray, Thos. W. B	1872

Murray, Wm. W	1876	Nourse, Miss Anna E	1881
Murray, Mrs. Laura A	1876	Nourse, Samuel Walker	1881
Murray, Mrs. L. W	1882		
Myers, Miss Emma	1881		
		O'Brien, Miss Nellie	1877
		Oburn, James M	1874
Nay, Mrs. Carrie S	1880	Offield, Mrs. Mary R	1878
Naylor, Mrs. Elizabeth A	1872	Olds, Chas. W	1881
Neahr, Mrs. Caroline W	1879	Olds, George D	1882
Nelson, Mrs. Mary J	1874	Oliver, John M	1871
Nelson, Julius	1877	Oliver, Mrs. Agnes S	1871
Nelson, Mrs. Augusta C	1877	Oliver, Mrs. Mary	1879
Nelson, Miss Mary	1881	Olmstead, Louis E	1878
Nelson, Miss Laura M	1882	Olmstead, Mrs. Catherine	1878
Nelson, Miss Florence M	1883	Olmstead, Kingsley R	1879
Nesbit, Mrs. Mary	1881	Olmstead, Miss Louise M	1880
New, Miss Emma	1877	O'Neall, Miss Hattie	1880
Newman, Dr. Henry P	1882	Onslow, Thos. T	1872
Newman, Mrs. Fannie L	1873	Oosterbeck, John M	1877
Newton, Henry S	1876	Oosterbeck, Mrs. Reinon	1877
Newton, Mrs. Ann H	1876	Oram, Miss Clara E	1883
Niblock, Frank	1878	Osborn, Wm	1856
Nichols, Gorton W	1872	Osborn, Miss Hattie J	1864
Nichols, Mrs. Annie M	1872	Osborn, Mrs. Susan	1873
Nichols, Mrs. Nettie	1876	Osborn, Henry A	1873
Nickels, E. O	1882	Osborn, Mrs. Anna C	1873
Nixon, Mrs. Leonora	1878	Osborn, Chauncey V	1882
Nolan, Mrs. Lucinda E	1879	Osborn, Mrs. Lydia D	1882
Nolan, Thos	1880	Osborne, Mrs. Jennie M	1880
Norton, Mrs. Sallie A	1867	Osborne, Miss Nellie White	1881
Norton, Miss Minnie M	1871	Oswald, John	1877
Norton, Henry M	1872	Ott, Mrs. Sarah	1881
Norton, S. E	1872	Ott, Mrs. Lydia	1882
Norton, Mrs. Jennie	1872	Oviatt, Frank F	1871
Norton, Horatio N	1876	Oviatt, Howard	1871
Norton, Mrs. H. N	1880	Oviatt, Mrs. Jesse L	1881
Nourse, Francis	1881	Owens, Mrs. Lizzie	1882
Nourse, Mrs. Sarah E	1881	Owsley, Harry B	1878

THIRD PRESBYTERIAN CHURCH.

Owsley, Mrs. Clara B.	1878	Peters, Miss Lena	1882
Owsley, Miss Emily	1879	Peterson, Miss Nellie	1879
Owsley, Miss Henriette E.	1880	Petterman, John L.	1878
Owsley, Fred. D.	1880	Pettibone, John H.	1880
Owsley, Geo. K.	1880	Pettit, James W.	1883
		Pettit, Mrs. Maria L.	1883
		Pettit, Miss Mary L.	1877
		Philip, Chas. R.	1881
Page, Chas. T.	1873	Philip, Mrs. Rosanna	1881
Painter, Mrs. Jane M.	1874	Phillips, Miss Hannah	1882
Palmer, Sophie M.	1873	Phillips, Miss Maud H.	1883
Park, Henry C.	1864	Pickands, Mrs. Louisa	1871
Park, Mrs. Mary	1864	Pierce, Mrs. A. M.	1878
Park, Mrs. Anna	1877	Pierce, Miss Nellie	1879
Parker, Mrs. Mary C.	1874	Pierce, Gerald A.	1879
Parker, Thos. J.	1877	Pierce, Paul	1881
Parry, Mrs. Martha A.	1882	Pierson, J. F.	1877
Partridge, Charles A.	1877	Pierson, Mrs. Jane L.	1877
Partridge, Mrs. Abbie L.	1878	Pierson, Geo. F.	1881
Patchin, Walter E.	1880	Pinto, Wm. H.	1878
Patterson, Mrs. Cornelia	1866	Pinto, Mrs. Henrietta B.	1878
Patterson, Mrs. Alice	1875	Pomeroy, Andrew J.	1876
Patterson, Wm. R.	1876	Pomeroy, Mrs. Lizzie W.	1876
Patterson, Sam'l E.	1879	Pond, Miss Anna	1880
Patterson, John	1880	Pool, Franklin	1882
Pattison, Jas.	1880	Pool, Mrs. Sarah R.	1882
Pattison, Mrs. Maggie E.	1880	Pope, Mrs. Jennie	1876
Patton, Miss Ella	1879	Porter, Fred. W.	1874
Patton, Wm. D.	1882	Porter, Mrs. Mary E.	1875
Paulson, Paul	1882	Porter, Miss Venona E.	1875
Payne, Walter D.	1873	Porter, Theodore	1877
Peck, Miss Emma A.	1874	Post, Mrs. Helen A. R.	1882
Pell, Wm. E.	1883	Post, Miss Sarah E.	1882
Pentacost, Miss Clara M.	1876	Post, Miss Maud	1882
Percy, Miss Jennie	1871	Post, Miss Anna	1882
Perry, Millard F.	1873	Potwin, Anson C.	1873
Perry, Mrs. Libby M.	1871	Potwin, Miss Anna E.	1873
Perry, John G.	1876	Poucher, Barent	1876
Perry, Mrs. Catherine	1876	Powell, Miss Carrie M.	1882

Pratt, Mrs. Anna M	1869	Rawson, Miss Ada	1865
Prentiss, Benjamin C	1874	Ray, Dr. J. E	1873
Prentiss, Mrs. Sarah F	1874	Ray, Mrs. Margaret	1873
Preston, Deming H	1871	Ray, William Augustus	1868
Preston, Mrs. Ella M	1871	Ray, Mrs. Susan C	1868
Preston, Mrs. Clarissa N	1879	Rea, James H	1875
Pribyl, Miss Pauline O	1878	Reddick, Miss Annie	1877
Pribyl, Joseph A	1879	Reddick, Miss Minnie J	1877
Pribyl, Ignatius M	1882	Redfield, Anson P	1881
Price, Robert	1876	Redfield, Mrs. Hattie A	1881
Price, Mrs. Mary A	1876	Redfield, Frank M	1881
Price, Miss Elizabeth	1876	Redfield, Miss Gertrude C	1881
Price, Miss Emily S	1876	Reed, Mrs. Margaret J	1876
Price, Wm. J	1877	Rees, George T	1877
Price, P. B	1880	Rees, Mrs. Sarah H	1877
Price, Mrs. Jennie C	1880	Reid, Mrs. Anna	1877
Price, Mrs. M. E	1882	Reid, Henry C	1877
Price, Mrs. Agnes	1882	Reid, Dr. Jas. G	1877
Pritchard, Daniel S	1876	Reid, John	1878
Protis, Chas	1877	Reid, Mrs. Isabella	1878
Purcell, Mrs. Adeline	1872	Reid, A. F	1882
Purcell, Miss Virginia B	1872	Reinhardt, Jacob H	1880
Purdy, Fred. B	1877	Remington, Mrs. Mary E	1882
Purington, James A	1882	Rendell, Miss Mary J	1881
Putnam, Mrs. Alida T	1873	Rennick, Miss Annie	1878
Putnam, Willard	1874	Reynolds, Miss Emma D	1877
		Reynolds, Miss Marion	1876
		Reynolds, Mrs. Mary E	1877
		Reynolds, Miss Matilda	1877
Quigg, Mrs. Francena	1878	Reynolds, Miss Maud M	1882
		Rice, Mrs. Elizabeth McL	1871
		Rice, Alonzo M	1872
		Rice, John F	1882
Ramsell, Mrs. Sylvina	1882	Rice, John A	1882
Randolph, Miss Frances	1874	Rice, Mrs. Elizabeth E	1882
Ransom, Edward S	1871	Rice, Miss Harriet M	1882
Rasmussen, Miss Olga M. M	1874	Rice, Mrs. Mary E	1882
Rasmussen, Mrs. Nathalia	1874	Rich, John M	1872
Rawson, Mrs. Emily B	1861	Rich, Albert R	1876

THIRD PRESBYTERIAN CHURCH.

Richey, Miss Mary	1874	Ross, Mrs. Alice	1882
Richey, Dr. W. S.	1874	Roth, Miss 'Mary A	1881
Richey, Mrs. Clara W	1875	Rowland, Miss Frances	1874
Richey, Miss Daisy B.	1877	Rowland, Miss Alice	1875
Richmond, Miss Myra V	1877	Rowland, Miss Mary	1875
Ridgway, Wm	1882	Rowland, Miss Clara A	1878
Rietz, Alex	1880	Rowland, Mrs. Mary C	1881
Riley, Mrs. Maud	1880	Runyan, Clark	1875
Rine, Elbridge	1877	Runyan, Mrs. Laura J	1875
Ring, Henry H	1876	Rutherford, Mr.	1875
Ring, Mrs. Elizabeth	1873	Rutherford, Mrs. Lucy A	1879
Robb, Mrs. Sarah L	1882	Russell, Miss Anna	1873
Roberts, Leon E	1877	Russell, Miss Marion	1877
Roberts, Mrs. Clara B	1877	Russell, Mrs. Minnie	1877
Roberts, Mrs. Ethalinda.	1882	Russell, Mrs. Sarah S	1878
Roberts, Miss Bertha	1882	Russell, Miss Nellie C	1879
Roberts, E. P	1882		
Roberts, Mrs. C. H	1882		
Robertson, Miss Jessie	1876		
Robertson, Wm. A	1877	Sabin, Sidney A	1882
Robertson, John.	1879	Sabin, Eugene F	1882
Robertson, Mrs. Christine C	1879	Salton, John	1878
Robinson, Joseph A	1873	Salton, Mrs. Emma	1878
Robinson, Mrs. Harriet S	1873	Samse, Miss Helen	1880
Robinson, Wm. T	1877	Sargent, Mrs. Elizabeth H	1881
Robinson, Mrs. Jennie M	1877	Sargent, John	1882
Robinson, Miss Hannah	1880	Sanders, Miss Kittie N	1878
Rockwell, Miss Lucy R	1878	Sanders, Milton S	1882
Rodgers, Gladstone K	1878	Savage, Miss Louise	1882
Rogan, Mrs. Mary J	1879	Scharr, William	1878
Rogers, Mrs. Kate G	1877	Schimmel, Wm. K	1876
Rommeiss, Miss Anna	1880	Schimmel, Miss Emma M	1876
Rommeiss, Miss Pauline	1881	Schimmel, Elam O	1876
Rommeiss, Miss Emma	1881	Schimmel, Mrs. E. O	1876
Ronstrom, Miss Ellen	1882	Schimmel, Miss Sallie	1877
Root, Miss Fannie A	1863	Schimmel, Miss Hannah	1877
Rose, Wm. J	1881	Schneider, Miss Emma R	1882
Rose, Chas. W	1882	Schmeltz, Mrs. Lizzie	
Ross, Hugh R	1882	Scholes, Parker	1876

THIRD PRESBYTERIAN CHURCH.

Schureman, Miss Lilian	1882
Schwarz, August	1875
Schwarz, Mrs. Dorothea	1875
Sclanders, Jas. L	1881
Scott, Robert	1866
Scott, Mrs. Sina	1873
Scott, George	1866
Scott, Miss Martha	1871
Scott, John Walls	1881
Sedgwick, Edwin H	1878
Sedgwick, Mrs. Virginia	1878
Sharp, Samuel	1873
Sharp, Mrs. Eliza	1873
Sharp, Miss Madgie L	
Sharp, Mrs. Margaret F	1879
Shaw, Miss Rebecca	1883
Shepherd, Miss Ellen	1880
Sherman, Geo. M	1877
Sherman, Miss Annie E	1877
Sherman, Miss Jennie	1878
Sherwood, Frederick W	1877
Shipman, Dr. George E	1866
Shipman, Mrs. Fanny	1800
Shipman, Frances C	1871
Shipman, Wm. J	1873
Shipman, Miss Margaret C	1875
Shipman, Geo. E. Jr	1875
Shipman, Wm. V	1880
Shipper, Miss Catharine	1876
Shoemaker, Miss Lizzie J	1880
Shoemaker, Miss Emma T	1880
Shoemaker, Miss Jessie M	1882
Shumway, Mrs. H. J	1862
Sibbald, Miss Emily	1880
Simpson, Miss Tilla A	1876
Simpson, Miss Harriet E	1876
Simpson, Miss Mary L	1876
Simpson, Thomas S	1877
Simpson, Mrs. Margaret	1877
Simpson, Miss Euphemia	1877
Simpson, Miss Mattie E	1883
Simpson, Joseph A	1883
Sinclair, Wm. H	1883
Skinner, Miss Elizabeth A	1875
Skinner, Miss Mary S	1882
Slabbyhand, Miss Mary	1876
Slater, Miss Hattie S	1880
Sloan, Mrs. Eliza A	1875
Sloan, Miss Ella M	1877
Sloat, Miss Barbara A	1882
Smith, Mrs. Elizabeth M	1868
Smith, Charles M	1871
Smith, Robert	1874
Smith, Mrs. Emma	1874
Smith, William	1874
Smith, Mrs. Christina	1875
Smith, Mrs. Mary	1876
Smith, Miss Laura A	1876
Smith, Miss Elizabeth L	1877
Smith, John K	1877
Smith, Mrs. Margaret D	1877
Smith, Miss Etta	1877
Smith, Eben B	1879
Smith, Mrs. Harriet	1879
Smith, Mrs. Cornelia H	1879
Smith, Dr. Wm. A	1879
Smith, Mrs. Rebecca M	1879
Smith, Jas. G	1881
Smith, E. W	1881
Smith, Mrs. Lucy	1881
Smith, Chas. H	1881
Smith, Frank R	1882
Smith, David R	1882
Smith, Fred'k H	1882
Snedden, James	1877
Snell, Joseph H	1879
Snitzler, John Henry	1872
Snitzler, Mrs. Maria	1872

THIRD PRESBYTERIAN CHURCH.

Name	Year	Name	Year
Snitzler, Miss Julia	1881	Stenhouse, Wm. B	1878
Snow, Mrs. Emma L	1882	Stephani, Miss Annie D	1874
Snyder, Mrs. A. H	1874	Stephens, Edward	1874
Snyder, Omer C	1881	Stephens, Mrs. Julia A	1874
Solomon, Henry	1877	Stephens, Mrs. Sarah H	1876
Spain, Miss Helen	1880	Stevens, Robbins E	1866
Spalding, Miss Harriet	1872	Stevens, Mrs. Betsey	1866
Speaber, Theodore	1874	Stevens, James F	1873
Spilman, Miss Florence	1879	Stevens, Mrs. Adelaide A	1875
Spilman, Mrs. Rebecca	1879	Stevens, Geo. C	1882
Spinck, John C. H	1875	Stevens, Mrs. Nellie B	1882
Spooner, Frank E	1873	Stevenson, Jabez E	1882
Spooner, Mrs. Maria P	1873	Stevenson, Mrs. Belle J. W	1882
Squair, Daniel	1877	Stewart, Mrs. Caroline	1875
Squires, Charles	1872	Stewart, Mrs. Mary	1876
Squires, Mrs. Mary B	1872	Stewart, Miss Margaret A	1878
Squires, Z	1873	Stewart, Miss Alice F	1879
Squires, Mrs. Harriet L	1873	Stewart, Miss Catharine J	1879
Squire, Harry F	1881	Stewart, Wm	1879
Staats, J. G	1881	Stewart, Mrs. Harriet A	1879
Staats, Mrs. Elizabeth	1882	Stewart, Jas	1880
Staats, Miss Jennie M	1882	Stewart, Miss Mary	1880
Staats, Henry N	1882	Stewart, Neil	1880
Stafford, Miss Ruth A	1880	Stewart, Mrs. Catherine	1880
Stagg, Robert	1877	Stewart, Miss Gertrude L	1881
Stagg, Mrs. Eliza	1877	Stewart, Henry	1881
Stagg, Miss Lydia J	1881	Stewart, Wm	1882
Stanton, Miss Maggie	1879	Stewart, Mrs. Ella	1882
Staples, Mrs. Amelia T	1881	St. John, Jean	1877
Statler, Stewart	1877	Stimpson, James M	1877
Statler, Mrs. Lida J	1877	Stimpson, Mrs. Theresa A	1877
Stattman, Miss Lillie F	1880	Stitt, Miss Maggie	1874
Steacy, Lewis E	1882	Stoddard, George B	1874
Stead, James H	1877	Stoddard, Mrs. E. Blanche	1874
Stead, Mrs. Cynthia D	1869	Storey, Mrs. Elizabeth	1874
Stead, Miss Minneiska	1876	Story, Harry T	1873
Stein, Miss Anna P	1881	Stratton, Mrs. Mary J	1878
Stein, Otto I	1883	Stratton, Miss Ladorna J	1877
Stelle, Mrs. Carrie E	1882	Stratton, Robert J	1877

THIRD PRESBYTERIAN CHURCH.

Stratton, Miss Sarah A......... 1877	Tebbetts, Arthur............... 1882
Strayer, Thos. A............... 1882	Telfer, Mrs. Agnes............. 1882
Strayer, Mrs. Grace L.......... 1882	Telfer, Thos. C................ 1882
Streich, Wm. F................. 1881	Telfer, Alex. R................ 1882
Streich, Henry F............... 1881	Templeton, Robert............. 1872
Streich, Fred. O............... 1882	Templeton, Herbert............ 1880
Strum, Adolph................. 1875	Templeton, Mrs. Mary.......... 1881
Stryker, Stephen W............ 1877	Templeton, Miss Mary.......... 1881
Stryker, Mrs. Annie E.......... 1877	Templeton, Wm. F.............. 1882
Stuart, John T................. 1877	Templeton, Mrs. Agnes......... 1882
Stuart, Mrs. Emily L........... 1877	Templeton, Miss Anna.......... 1882
Stuart, Joseph................. 1878	Templeton, Miss Maggie W..... 1883
Stuart, Mrs. Letitia............ 1878	Templeton, Miss Evelyn........ 1883
Suter, Alexander............... 1875	Templeton, Clifford F.......... 1883
Suter, Arthur.................. 1882	Tennant, Richard W............ 1882
Sutton, Mrs. Josephine A....... 1880	Terkurst, Miss Minnie.......... 1880
Swan, Miss Mary E............. 1881	Terkurst, Miss Sinna G......... 1880
Swartz, Mrs. Maggie F......... 1877	Terkurst, Miss Hattie........... 1880
Swett, Mrs. Laura R............ 1878	Terwiliger, Geo. W............. 1877
Swett, Leonard Herbert........ 1880	Terwiliger, Maynard............ 1877
Swingley, Allen A.............. 1883	Thiel, Miss Ida C............... 1881
Swonson, Henry................ 1873	Thomas, Mrs. Sarah............ 1872
Swonson, Mrs. Ella W.......... 1873	Thomas, Jas. W................ 1873
Symington, Wm. J............. 1874	Thomas, James................. 1875
	Thomas, Miss Anna............ 1875
	Thomas, Miss Elizabeth A...... 1876
	Thomas, Wm. H. H............ 1880
Tallmadge, John H............. 1883	Thomas, Mrs. Caroline A....... 1880
Tallmadge, Mrs. Mary C........ 1883	Thomas, Miss Cora............. 1880
Tallmadge, Miss Florence....... 1883	Thomas, Albert R.............. 1880
Talcott, Wm................... 1872	Thomas, Mrs. Brescia.......... 1880
Tanner, Miss Hattie M.......... 1880	Thomas, Miss Helen B.......... 1880
Taylor, Mrs. Elizabeth L........ 1879	Thomson, James................ 1875
Taylor, James 1883	Thompson, Mark S............. 1873
Taylor, Mrs. Eliza.............. 1883	Thompson, Mrs. Emma L....... 1878
Taylor, Miss Annie............. 1883	Thompson, Mrs. Sarah C....... 1876
Teall, Edward M............... 1863	Throop, Mrs. Ann E............ 1851
Teall, Mrs. Kate................ 1863	Tichenor, Lyman B............. 1876
Teall, Henry D................. 1871	Tilden, Edward................ 1882

THIRD PRESBYTERIAN CHURCH.

Tobin, Moses	1876	Van Ness, John Q	1875
Tombs, Miss Jennie H	1877	Van Ness, Mrs. Clara	1875
Townsend, G. B	1881	Van Ness, John F	1880
Townsend, Mrs. Carrie	1881	Van Ness, Miss Anna A	1880
Townsend, Miss Mary E	1882	Van Nortwick, John S	1877
Travis, J. A	1880	Van Orden, Mrs. Sarah	1877
Treleaven, Miss Mary A	1872	Varney, Gorham C	1870
Treleaven, Albert	1877	Varney, Mrs. Caroline C	1870
Treleaven, Mrs. Jennie	1877	Varney, Luther H	1877
True, Mrs. Corinne	1878	Vermaas, Peter M	1881
Trimingham, Miss Ann E	1857	Vermaas, Cornelius	1881
Trimingham, Ralph N	1858	Vernon, Mrs. Wm	1882
Trimingham, Miss Frances M	1858	Vix, Mrs. Sarah J	1879
Trunkey, Mrs. Ida I	1876		
Tuthill, Wm. H	1880		
Tuthill, Mrs. Sophia B	1880		
Tuthill, Frank H	1881	Wade, Mrs. Charlotte D	1876
Tuthill, Miss Eva	1881	Wadsworth, Mrs. Bertha	1874
Tuttle, Miss Bertha M	1879	Waldron, Miss Virginia E	1881
		Waldron, Abraham	1882
		Waldron, Mrs. Mary E	1882
		Walker, William	1877
Underhill, Mrs. Carrie E	1876	Walker, Miss Emilie S	1879
Upperdahl, John	1876	Walker, Mrs. Emma E	1879
		Walker, Oshea	1881
		Walker, Mrs. Hannah A	1881
		Walker, Miss Olivett M	1881
Van Bershot, John	1873	Walker, Sylvester	1881
Van Bershot, Mrs. Jacomine	1873	Walker, Jas. P	1881
Van Bershott, Miss Hattie	1880	Walker, Mrs. Maria R	1881
Van Buskirk, Mrs. Elizabeth	1879	Walker, George R	1883
Van Buskirk, Miss Estella	1879	Waller, Henry	1871
Van de Roovaart, Jacob	1880	Waller, Edward C	1871
Van de Roovaart, Mrs. Elizabeth	1880	Waller, Mrs. Mary L	1873
Van Dusen, Arthur S	1880	Waller, Miss Sarah Bell L	1877
Van Es, Mitchell M	1879	Wallis, Mrs. Janet M	1871
Van Es, Mrs. Mary P	1879	Walters, James	1876
Van Housen, Mrs. Frances M	1881	Walters, Miss Elizabeth McL	1882
Valentine, John	1881	Ward, Miss Agnes E	1880

Ward, Mrs. Janet	1880	Westerman, Mrs. Augusta E.	1880
Ward, Miss Helen M.	1880	Whallon, Mrs. Harriet S.	1881
Ware, Miss Nellie S.	1879	Wheadon, Seth	1871
Ware, Alex. C.	1882	Wheadon, Mrs. Phœbe A.	1865
Warner, Wm. C.	1868	Wheadon, Miss Alice A.	1875
Warner, Mrs. Emily C.	1876	White, Mrs. Agnes A.	1872
Warner, Miss Ella M.	1881	White, Miss Lizzie D.	1877
Warner, Miss Mary W.	1880	Whitley, Miss Mary	1871
Warner, Miss Mattie H.	1882	Whiteside, Henry	1873
Waring, Miss Henrietta A.	1879	Whiting, Chas. H.	1881
Washburn, Miss Julia M.	1875	Whiting, Mrs. Frank C.	1881
Washburn, Mrs. Jane C.	1875	Whitman, Henry R.	1877
Waters, Wm. H.	1875	Whitman, Wm. F.	1877
Waters, Mrs. Sarah J.	1875	Whitman, Mrs. Laura J.	1877
Waters, John	1880	Whitson, Mrs. Ann	1882
Waterhouse, Miss Maud H.	1882	Whitson, Miss Jennie E.	1882
Watson, Artemas D.	1875	Whitson, Robt. J.	1881
Watson, Mrs. Catherine	1875	Whiton, Miss Emma L.	1873
Webb, James	1869	Wilbur, J. H.	1881
Webb, Mrs. Mary	1869	Wilbur, Mrs. Mary H.	1881
Webb, Wm. E.	1873	Wilbur, Miss Josephine	1881
Webb, Mrs. Charlotte J.	1873	Wilcox, Mrs. Mary C.	1876
Webb, Mrs. Mary	1874	Wilcox, Mrs. Celuda	1881
Webb, Mrs. M. J.	1876	Wilcox, Frederick W.	1882
Webber, Mrs. Hannah F.	1880	Wilkinson, Mrs. Arvilla E.	1873
Webster, Mrs. Ida N.	1876	Will, Charles	1876
Webster, Miss Sarah	1876	Will, Mrs. Lizzie	1876
Webster, Miss Kittie	1876	Williams, Mrs. Mary	1872
Weigley, Frank S.	1880	Williams, Mrs. D.	1874
Weigley, Mrs. Emily S.	1880	Williams, Miss Martha	1874
Wells, Wheeler W.	1879	Williams, Miss Sarah M.	1874
Wells, Mrs. Nancy	1879	Williams, Miss Mary J.	1875
Wells, Miss Florence	1880	Williams, Miss Margaret	1875
Wells, Miss Anna P.	1881	Williams, Mrs. Mary	1875
Wells, Mrs. Cherrill H.	1882	Williams, Miss Jessie M.	1878
Welsh, Mrs. Rosanna S.	1876	Williams, Miss Annie E.	1878
Wendtz, Mrs. Susie	1878	Williams, Miss Amelia H.	1879
Wentworth, Mrs. Mary A.	1877	Williams, Benj. J.	1882
West, Mrs. Catherine A.	1883	Williams, Edwin C.	1882

Williamson, Norman J	1877	Wood, Mrs. Jane L	1862
Williamson, Mrs. Maria D	1881	Wood, David W	1876
Williamson, Samuel S	1881	Wood, Mrs. Jennie	1882
Williamson, Mrs. Martha A	1881	Wood, Mrs. Mary E	1878
Williamson, Miss Mary	1881	Woodbury, Mrs. Hattie F	1881
Wilmot, Thos	1879	Woodcock, Lindsay T	1881
Wilmot, Mrs. Phœbe	1879	Woodworth, Mrs. Emma	1878
Wilmot, Miss Jane	1881	Woolf, W. H	1879
Wilson, Miss Margaret R	1872	Woolf, Mrs. Harriet E	1879
Wilson, Miss May F	1878	Work, Mrs. Mary A	1879
Wilson, Miss Sophy Lou	1878	Work, Samuel J	1879
Wilson, Mrs. Eliza	1878	Wormer, Mrs. Frank A	1872
Wilson, Miss Lida M	1878	Worthington, Mrs. Ella L	1871
Wilson, John	1879	Wright, Junius P	1877
Wilson, Miss Anna M	1879	Wright, Miss Clara L	1879
Wilson, Mrs. Lavinia P	1879	Wyllie, James T	1882
Wilson, Archibald H	1881	Wynkoop, Mrs. Catherine A	1882
Wilson, George A. S	1883	Wysong, Mrs. Hannah	1877
Wilson, Mrs. Alice M	1883		
Wilson, Mrs. Malvina M	1883		
Wilt, Chas. D	1877		
Wing, Miss Annie E	1874	Yates, Miss Frances L	1860
Winloff, Nels	1877	Yaggy, Levi W	1880
Winn, Mrs. Charlotte B	1874	York, Miss Emma	1878
Winter, Mrs. Minerva	1872	Young, Wm. F	1876
Winter, Hugh A	1875	Young, Mrs. Jennet	1876
Winter, Frank P	1880	Young, Miss Margaret A	1876
Winters, Robert A	1878	Young, William	1876

SUPPLEMENT.

MANUAL

THIRD PRESBYTERIAN CHURCH,

CHICAGO, ILLINOIS.

May, 1883–1884.

OFFICERS.

PASTOR.
Rev. ABBOTT E. KITTREDGE, D.D.

ASSISTANT PASTOR.
Rev. W. S. POST, D.D.

ELDERS.

SAMUEL M. MOORE.	DAVID BRADLEY.
CHAS. L. CURRIER.	LOTHROP S. HODGES.
LOUIS F. BURRELL.	JAS. P. KETCHAM.
EDWARD M. TEALL.	THOS. KANE.
JAS. A. HAIR.	DEMING H. PRESTON.
FRANK E. SPOONER.	JAMES SUYDAM KNOX.
ALBERT G. BEEBE.	HENRY A. OSBORN.
LEVI W. YAGGY.	BENJAMIN C. PRENTISS.
ANDREW M. HENDERSON.	THOS. GOODMAN, Treas.

RALPH N. TRIMINGHAM, Clerk.

DEACONS.

JOHN H. SNITZLER.	LINDSAY T. WOODCOCK.
WM. D. MESSINGER.	ALBERT B. CLARK.
JAS. S. HUBBARD.	JOSHUA EMERY.

WM. H. BEEBE.

TRUSTEES.

DAVID BRADLEY, Pres.	THOS. N. BOND.
ROBT. SCOTT.	JAS. A. HAIR.
FRANK E. SPOONER.	LOTHROP S. HODGES.
CHAS. L. CURRIER.	A. J. HARDING.

JAMES P. KETCHAM, Treas.

USHERS.

JAMES A. HAIR.	JOHN WALLS SCOTT.
JOSHUA EMERY.	LOUIS L. MUNSON.
ALBERT B. CLARK.	WM. A. GOODMAN.
GEORGE MORGAN.	MORGAN K. DEALE.
CHAS. D. MILL.	JOHN F. RICE.
THOS. A. STRAYER.	A. W. BURKHARDT.

SEXTON.
PRATT HAMILTON.

SUNDAY SCHOOLS.

HOME.
MEETS AT 2.30 P.M.

OFFICERS.

ALBERT G. BEEBE.....................	Superintendent.
WM. A. GOODMAN.... ⎫	
JOSHUA EMERY....... ⎬	Assistant Superintendents.
BENJ. C. PRENTISS ... ⎭	
E. H. COOK...........................	Sup't Primary Dept.
LOUIS L. MUNSON.....................	Assistant.
CHAS. D. MILL........................	Secretary and Treasurer.
SEYMOUR MORRIS......................	Assistant.
FREDRICK W. WILCOX..................	Librarian.
J. HOHMANN..........................	Assistant.
M. E. JOHNSTON	Reception Committee.

MEMBERSHIP OF THE SCHOOL, APRIL 1, 1884.

Primary Pupils 246	Teachers.............22		
Junior " 370	" 40		
Senior " 257	" 26		
Bible Class Pupils 239	" 7		
Total Membership —		—	1236
Average Attendance for the year			838$\frac{3}{8}$
Largest " in "			1026
Smallest " " "			482
Balance brought forward May 1, 1883..................		$	276 59
Total contributions during the year...................			1,045 72
			$1,322 31

The following sums have been donated by the School, viz:

To Foreign Missions ....$	349	78
Also to Miss Powers, in Turkey........................	100	00
To Capt. Bundy, Gospel Ship	50	00
" Church at Eureka Springs, Ark. (Communion Service)..	21	20
For Funeral flowers	40	00
" Sick person in Woman's Hospital	50	00
" Church Industrial School	147	55
" Church at Lawrenceburgh, Ind. (injured by Ohio flood)	58	88
" Cook Co. S. S. Association	50	00
Christmas festival, Foster Mission	36	29
" " Noble street Mission	36	28
To Northwestern Theological Seminary, for Organ.........	25	00
" Presbyterian Church, Flandreau, Dak.................	25	00
" Free Kindergarten, Halsted street...................	50	00
" Rev. Mr. Young, Boys' School, Alaska	50	00
" Home for the Friendless, City	50	00
" Deacon's fund to aid poor families not connected with our Church	100	00
" Women's and Children's Hospital	23	24
Balance carried forward.............................	59	09
	$1,322	31
Scholars received into the church during the year 1883		57

FOSTER MISSION,

MASKELL HALL, No. 173 DESPLAINES STREET,

MEETS AT 2:30 P. M.

OFFICERS:

JAMES S. HUBBARD	Superintendent.
HENRY H. MORGAN JAMES P. KETCHAM	Assistant Superintendents.
JAMES H. MILES	Secretary and Treasurer.
WILLIAM T. TEMPLETON	Sup't Inft. Class.
THOMAS KANE	Ass't Sup't Inft. Class.
DAVID W. WOOD	Teacher Bible Class.
SAMUEL W. KEMPSTER	Librarian.

ABBREVIATED REPORT OF FOSTER MISSION.

Total enrollment	754
Average attendance in 1883	388
Smallest attendance in 1883, January 21	226
Largest attendance in 1883, December 19	542
Number of teachers and officers	45

TREASURER'S REPORT.

Balance on hand January 1, 1883	$ 21 79	
Sabbath collections	314 85	
Home school contribution	36 29	
Received for entertainment	9 72	
		$382 65

EXPENSES.

Papers, etc., for school	$231 88	
Sundry items	31 50	
Christmas festival	95 90	
Entertainment	15 00	
Balance on hand January 1, 1884	8 37	
		$382 65

In addition to the above, the Third church contributed $450 00 for rent of the hall and other expenses.

The Infant Class numbers from 100 to 175 children, and the Bible Class from 30 to 50 members. In connection with the latter a weekly Prayer meeting is held.

The location of this school is unfortunate, both for its growth and prosperity, held in a hall in a third story, inaccessible to children, and under the shadow of a Catholic church, not favorable to its prosperity with many of the children living a long distance south. The necessity seems apparent that the school, for its own usefulness, should be located south of Van Buren or Harrison streets.

JAMES H. MILES, Secretary.

NOBLE-STREET MISSION.

OFFICERS.

Daniel Forbes..................Superintendent.
W. H. Beebe ....Assistant Superintendent.
Geo. E. Shipman...............Secretary and Assistant Treasurer.
A. M. Henderson ....Treasurer.
Miss F. C. Shipman.............Superintendent Infant Department.

SECRETARY'S REPORT.

From May 1, 1883, to May 1, 1884:

Total attendance during the year	17,123
Largest " " " "	465
Smallest " " " "	302
Average attendance for the year	330
Number of teachers and officers	34
Number of scholars received into the Church	12

TREASURER'S REPORT.

RECEIPTS.

Balance brought forward	$3	13
Collections for the year	208	53
Donation from Home School	36	28
Collected for Christmas Entertainment	75	50
Total	$323	44

DISBURSEMENTS.

Cook County Sunday School Association	$5	73
Foreign Sunday School Association	51	00
American Sunday School Union	50	00
Half Orphan Asylum	52	46
Foundlings' Home	52	47
Christmas Entertainment	111	78
Total	$323	44

REPORT OF THE TREASURER OF THE SESSION.

Payments made from May 1, 1883, to May 1, 1884, by Thomas Goodman, Treasurer of the Session.

Balance in the Treasury May 1, 1883..........................		$248.70
Received in Collections for the following causes:		
For Sunday School Work................................$4,319 39		
" Home Missions..	884 78	
" Foreign Missions...............	1,510 89	
" Gospel on the Lakes..................................	50 00	
" Church Erection.......................................	337 31	
" Sustentation..	112 45	
" Bible Society..	38 30	
" Boards of the Church.................................	1,076 35	
" General Fund..	510 71	8,840 18
Total...		$9,088 88

DISBURSEMENTS AS FOLLOWS:

To Sunday School Work, including Home and Mission Schools..$4,161 12		
" Home Missions.......................................	1,014 07	
" Foreign Missions...................	1,726 50	
" Gospel on the Lakes..................................	50 00	
" Church Erection.......................................	377 05	
" Sustentation..	146 89	
" Bible Society..	55 97	
" Aid for Colleges........................	130 29	
" Ministerial Relief......................................	42 39	
" Freedmen...	42 39	
" Education...	14 12	
" Publication Society................................... ...	14 13	
" General Assembly................................	192 86	
" Church Manuals......................................	212 00	
" Trustees of the Church.........	176 61	
" Funeral Expenses, Flowers, etc., at Funerals of Ruling Elders.	77 50	
" Printing, Stationery, Postage, etc.........................	68 75	
" Eastman & Fiske for Hotel Registers.....................	10 00	
" Manuals of Chicago Presbytery..........................	6 00	
" Sundry items..	61 35	
		8,579 99
Balance in the Treasury May 1, 1884........................		508 89
Total...........		$9,088 88

THOMAS GOODMAN, Treasurer.

THE BOARD OF DEACONS.

The Board of Deacons is organized with the Pastor as Moderator for the purpose of overseeing the poor of the Church in visitation and relief. An additional duty is the care of the communion service, and of providing for the communion table. They also have under their care the church burial-lot at Rose Hill, which is entirely paid for, and upon which they expect to erect a suitable monument at an early day.

A regular meeting of the Board is held on the second Friday of each month; at which the Treasurer renders a report of receipts and expenditures. At the same time, reports are made by the different members of the Board, as to cases left in their charge. New cases are then brought to the attention of the Board, and such measures taken for their investigation and relief as may be deemed necessary. Great care is taken in extending assistance, and the unanimous assent of at least three members must be obtained before any pecuniary relief can be rendered.

The resources of the Board are obtained from the Sacramental collections, which are set apart for the relief of the poor of the Church, and from occasional special collections.

The work of the Board for the past year has been carried on faithfully and quietly; but we believe not unfruitfully, and to the honor of the Savior's name. Pecuniary aid has been extended to seventeen families and individuals during the year, which includes funeral expenses in several instances.

In accordance with the custom of the Board, a large number of turkeys and other necessaries were distributed amongst our Church poor on Thanksgiving Day.

We trust that our Church membership will during the coming year contribute even more liberally to the funds of this Board, as there is practically no limit to the good that can be done, if only the necessary means are made available.

During the past year, our dear friend and fellow-laborer, A. Hoffman Keese, has been called from the service below to that of the Church above, being the first from our number to pass through the gates into the City. The Board unanimously passed the following resolutions:

WHEREAS, God in His Providence, on the twelfth of March, 1884, called from our number our dear brother and Secretary, A. HOFFMAN KEESE,

Resolved, That we as a Board do hereby testify to his great Christian worth, his devotion to the Master's cause, his zeal in every good work, his earnestness and consecration as evinced in his daily walk, and to our high appreciation of his faithful and valuable services as a member and Secretary of this Board.

By his death we have lost an efficient and earnest fellow-laborer, and the Church a most useful member.

Resolved, That we extend our heartfelt sympathy to the family in their bereavement, and that these resolutions be placed upon the records of this Board, and copies be transmitted to his wife and mother.

WM. H. BEEBE, SEC.

THIRD PRESBYTERIAN CHURCH.

Report of the Treasurer of the Board of Deacons for the year commencing April 1, 1883, and ending March 31, 1884:

RECEIPTS.

Balance on hand March 31, 1883	$158	99
Sacramental collection for April, 1883	126	80
" " " June, 1883	139	77
" " " August, 1883	56	00
" " " October, 1883	142	33
" " " December, 1883	123	85
" " " January, 1884	106	10
" " " February, 1884	135	42
Thanksgiving collection from Wednesday evening meeting, November 28, 1883	66	41
Thanksgiving collection	126	83
Emma New, donation	3	30
Money refunded Board	1	50
	$1,187	30

DISBURSEMENTS

From April 1, 1883, to March 31, 1884:

General relief	$393	75
Funeral expenses	104	00
Bread and wine for communion	43	01
Paid Treasurer of session for manuals	69	88
Miscellaneous expenses	6	75
Thanksgiving dinners for poor families	40	79
Sinking fund for Monument	200	00
Foundlings' Home, one-half Thanksgiving collection	60	91
Women's Christian Association, one-half Thanksgiving collection	60	92
Balance on hand March 31, 1884	207	29
	$1,187	30

J. H. SNITZLER, Treasurer.

DEACON'S CONTINGENT FUND

For assisting those who are not members of the Church:

RECEIPTS.

January 24, received from Treasurer of Sabbath-school..	$100 00

DISBURSEMENTS.

General relief	$19 25
Balance on hand March 31, 1884	80 75
	$100 00

MONUMENT FUND.

RECEIPTS.

Set aside from Deacon's Fund	$200 00

DISBURSEMENTS.

Balance on hand March 31, 1884	$200 00

J. H. SNITZLER, Treasurer.

REPORT OF TREASURER OF TRUSTEES.

RECEIPTS.

Balance on hand	$ 1,579 21
Received from Pew Rents	18,242 02
" " Collections	3,594 25
" " Other Sources.................	3,550 88
	$26,966 36

EXPENDITURES.

Paid Pastor's Salary.........................	$ 8,000 00
" For Music.............................	3,238 45
" Interest on Bonded Debt................	1,200 00
Gift to Westminster Church..................	4,900 00
Paid for Insurance on Church Property	432 50
" Janitor and Assistant	1,410 00
" for Gas	416 80
" " Fuel.............................	602 16
" " Pulpit Supply—Pastor's Vacation	400 00
" " Printing Sermons and Leaflets........	1,214 25
" " Repairs to Church Building, etc......	1,456 32
" " Sundry Expenses	3,228 87
	$26,499 35
Balance on hand......................	467 01
	$26,966 36

LADIES' BENEVOLENT WORK.

MRS. W. H. ANDERSON, PRESIDENT; MRS. WM. MENDSEN, VICE-PRESIDENT.

The Ladies' Benevolent Society reorganized October 23, 1883. There has been held, during the season, ten meetings, four of which convened at 11 o'clock, and were made interesting and entertaining by reports from various charitable and benevolent societies; also readings and religious exercises, after which a lunch was served. The remaining six were devoted entirely to work, and met at the usual hour. The largest attendance has been 135; the smallest, 45. Individual contributions of material have been received, valued at $35; also 400 second-hand garments.

Special purchases have been made from the society fund, amounting to $90, which were equal to 100 pieces.

The above 400 articles, with the 500 made by the united efforts of the ladies, makes a total of 900 pieces. From these, four boxes have been compiled and sent away, two to Park College, Mo., and two to home missionaries; the approximate value of them being $265. The remainder were distributed in our city, as follows:

The Northwestern Theological Seminary; Illinois Industrial School for Girls; Home for Incurables; Foundlings' Home, and some fifty families of our worthy poor. Our season closed March 26, with a membership of 88. As our reports stand, may we not feel amply repaid for the time given, and cheered by the sacred words, "Cast thy bread upon the waters, for thou shalt find it after many days."

Treasurer's Report.

Balance in Treasury from last year	$ 2	50
Received from Benevolent Fund of the Church	250	00
" " Membership Fees	47	00
" " Special contributions	33	00
Total	$332	50

DISBURSEMENTS.

Paid Park College, Mo	$ 6	00
" A. C. Stark, Iowa	21	00
" Sick woman	14	00
" Mattress for Y.M.C.A. room	10	00
" Incidental expenses of the society	25	75
" Drayage and freight on boxes	4	50
" Mrs. Anderson, Pres., for the purchase of material	251	25
Total	$332	50

Mrs. C. H. Chappell, Sec. and Treas.

INDUSTRIAL SCHOOL.

OFFICERS.

Mrs. A. G. Beebe .... Superintendent.
Mrs. P. B. Price .... Assistant Superintendent.
Mrs. E. T. Davis.......... Superintendent of Work.
Mrs. J. P. Mills .... Secretary and Treasurer.
Miss Hattie Rice.......... Superintendent of Primary Department.

The School opened October 13, 1883, at the Temperance Church, on Noble street, with an attendance of 176 scholars. By November 15, the number had increased until no more scholars could be received, and December 1st the School was removed to a larger church, where there has been a

Total Enrollment ....347 scholars
Average Attendance..............................272 "
Smallest   "   October 13......................176 "
Largest   "   February 16 ....307 "
Total Enrollment .... 36 teachers
Average Attendance.............................. 26 "
Smallest   "   .... 6 "
Largest   "   .... 31 "

The girls under instruction in this school are from five to fifteen years of age, and of eight nationalities, and have been found to be teachable and obedient, and during the two hours each Saturday spent in the Schools, have made great progress in sewing, also in their appearance, special attention having been given to cultivating cleanliness and ladylike behavior, as well as teaching the foundations of the Christian faith, and endeavoring to lead them to Jesus as their Savior and Guide.

There have been completed in the School during the past winter 374 garments and 240 tidies, the latter being used as preparatory to garments by beginners, in connection with patchwork.

Collections have been taken in the School every Saturday, amounting in all to $34.17, which, with $147.55 given by the Home Sunday School, has been used to defray the expenses of the School.

The thing standing in the way of the highest usefulness of this School is the want of a sufficient number of faithful teachers, though there is an increased interest in this department of the ladies' work, and we hope another year may find many more of our sisters ready to *sacrifice* something to be used by the Master in this work of bringing some of the heathen at our own doors, both to knowledge of civilized living and to Christ, by helping these girls to become useful, Christian women.

THE WOMAN'S FOREIGN MISSIONARY SOCIETY.

The annual meeting in March brought another year's work to a close making thirteen years since this society was organized. The following ladies were elected officers for the ensuing year: President, Miss L. R. Hall; vice-presidents, Mrs. H. T. Helm, Mrs. A. E. Kittredge, Mrs. L. S. Hodges, Dr. Emma Woodworth; Treasurer, Mrs. H. A. Osborn; Finance Committee, Mrs. J. P. Ketcham, Mrs. Lockwood, Mrs. R. I. Adamson; secretary, Mrs. J. P. Mills.

Our society numbers over 250 members, and has never seemed more prosperous, or sustained by more efficient workers than at the present time.

Meetings have been held during the year on the third Tuesday of each month at 3 P.M., in the church parlors. The general subjects recommended by the Board have been taken up and discussed. Letters have been received from all parts of the missionary field. The opportunity of listening to Mrs. Van Hook, of Persia, and others returned from their missionary labors for a little rest, has been offered to us on several occasions. We have also had the pleasure of welcoming to our society Mrs. Hoge, president of the Woman's Board of the Northwest. Her earnest spiritual words have been a help, and an inspiration to us in pushing forward the work.

We have renewed our pledges for the support of Mrs. Kelso and Miss Olmsted for the coming year. Mrs. Kelso is again engaged in her lifework in her beloved India. She writes of having been transferred from Lahore to Saharanpur. Her letters are full of interest as her own noble life is full of labor for the Master. Mrs. Olmsted, who is in Siam, devotes much of her time teaching in the girls' school at Bangkok. Her knowledge of medicine gives her opportunities for doing untold good.

We know that her life is consecrated to the service of Christ, and that *whatsoever* her hands find to do will be done to His honor and glory. The work of the year has been in several respects unusually pleasant and encouraging. Both officers and members have labored together earnestly and harmoniously, and have not been without the reward which such association in Christian work is sure to bring.

Our society has grown to be one of the regular church activities, but our constant prayer is that every sister in the church may arise, and, in the strength of her spiritual energies and intellectual endowments, place this work on a higher plane than it has yet attained to, or ever can reach until an interest is felt and evinced, not by the few or the majority, but by *all*. We cannot forbear to make mention of the praise meeting, held under the auspices of our society, on the afternoon of February 28, that "great day of the feast," when, in response to the invitation "Bring an offering and come into His Courts," the "tithes were brought into the storehouse," and a blessing was poured out upon us. Hymns of praise were sung; psalms of thanksgiving were read; prayers of consecration were offered; glowing words came from consecrated hearts and lips, and offerings of praise were laid at His feet. As we turned our steps from the church door, these words seemed borne on every passing breeze, "Bless the Lord, Oh my soul, and all that is within me bless His holy name," and the response came back to every heart who had offered a gift, "Inasmuch as ye have done it unto one of the least of these, ye have done it unto me."

Let us not be discouraged, for the work is the Lord's; but be thankful that He permits us to have a share, not only in the work, but in the reward, listening to His words, "Be not weary in well doing, for in due season ye shall reap if ye faint not." But though *we faint*, the work of Foreign Missions will still go on, for Christ died for *all*, and the "glad tidings" will be sent throughout the length and breadth of the whole wide world, until every knee shall bow before Him, and every heart shall acknowledge the name of Christ as their Redeemer.

Mrs. J. P. Mills, Secretary.

Report of the Treasurer of the Woman's Foreign Missionary Society for the year ending March 31, 1884.

RECEIPTS.

Balance in the Treasury	$ 144	07
Pledges due before April 1, 1883	43	90
Pledges paid for the year ending March 31, 1884	1,223	73
Thank-offerings received at the Praise Meeting	243	00
Collections	7	71
	$1,662	41

DISBURSEMENTS.

Gift to Miss Cummings	$150	00
Printing and postage for Praise Meeting	15	90
Fund for Presbyterial expenses	12	90
Miss Olmsted's salary	450	00
Mrs. Kelso's salary	400	00
Woman's Presbyterian Board of Missions	620	00
Miscellaneous expenses	8	20
	1,657	00
Balance in the Treasury	5	41
	$1,662	41

Mrs. H. A. Osborn, Treasurer.

YOUNG LADIES' BENEVOLENT SOCIETY.

This Society was organized purely for benevolent work.

The year 1883-4 opened with Mrs. A. G. Ashley, President; Mrs. R. J. Adamson, Vice-President; Miss Carrie B. Havens, Secretary; Miss Louise Savage, Treasurer.

During the preceding year $300 had been raised, and it was the first work of the society with this sum to provide a home for an old lady in the Old Ladies' Home of this city. The number of members this year, both active and associate, was 112. $408.52 was the total amount raised during the year. Of this $303.65 was disbursed by different committees in their work of visiting and aiding the Hospital for Women and Children, the Cook County Hospital, the Home for Incurables, one sick lady, and eight poor families. $25 was donated to the temperance work under the auspices of the Y. W. C. T. U., of the West Side, leaving in the treasury for the ensuing year the balance of $104.87.

SEED SOWERS.

The society called the Seed Sowers is composed of little girls from six to twelve years of age. There are sixty members, with an average attendance of thirty.

The children meet once in two weeks. They have supported, the past year, a little boy in Lodiana, India. The money was raised by a sale of fancy articles made by the little girls, and also from mission boxes, which each child has at home.

The society was very successful this last year, under the care of Mrs. B. C. Prentiss.

YOUNG PEOPLE'S LIBRARY ASSOCIATION.

OFFICERS.

L. T. WOODCOCK	President.
C. D. MILL	Vice-President.
M. E. JOHNSTON	Secictary.
SEYMOUR MORRIS	Treasurer.

During the year ending May 1, 1884, there have been added to the Library 376 volumes, of which number 359 were library books, in the strict sense of that term, and 17 were bound volumes of magazines and other periodicals; so that the library now contains about 1300 volumes. There were also added to the number of magazines and periodicals for the reading-room sixteen weekly papers; so that there are now on the tables of the reading-room, for the use of the young people of the church and congregation, thirty-three different newspapers, magazines and periodicals, including some of the best British and American publications of the kind.

Since the 1st of January of this year a new catalogue has been prepared, the library has been entirely rearranged, and it is to-day in perfect order and good condition.

The Association numbers 404 members.

Treasurer's Report of the Young People's Library Association.

RECEIPTS.

Balance on hand May 1, 1883		$ 107 56
Received for Initiation Fees and Dues	$393 00	
" " Tickets to Sociables	8 00	
" " Net Proceeds Lecture course	680 79	
" " Fines	37 72	
		1,119 51
		$1,227 07

DISBURSEMENTS.

Paid for Books, Periodicals, etc	$564 25	
" " Sociables.............................	147 78	
" " Binding, Printing, Stationery, etc	315 29	
		$1,027 32
Balance on hand		$ 199 75

CONDENSED STATEMENT

OF THE BENEVOLENCE OF THE CHURCH FOR THE YEAR.

Home Sunday School		$1,045 72
Foster Mission Sunday School		360 77
Noble-street Mission Sunday School		320 31
Industrial School		34 17
Treasurer of Session		8,840 18
"	Board of Deacons	1,028 31
"	Ladies' Foreign Missionary Society	1,518 34
"	Ladies' Benevolent Society	330 00
"	Young People's Library Association	1,119 51
"	Young Ladies' Benevolent Society	408 52
To this may be added the receipts by the Board of Trustees		25,387 15
Total		$40,392 98

In Memoriam.

Mrs. Mary B. Hale..........................January 14th, 1883.
Mrs. Claudine Daniels ....May 11th, 1883.
Miss Jennie A. Crane ....June 1st, 1883.
Daniel Squair ....June 22d, 1883.
Mrs. Jennet Young.............................July 23d, 1883.
Addison B. Heffling..........................August 12th, 1883.
Mrs. Catherine Stewart..................`.....September 19th, 1883.
John F. W. Macdonald......................October 9th, 1883.
John S. Carpenter ....November 12th, 1883.
Charles F. Chessman ....November 19th, 1883.
Willard Putnam ....December 1st, 1883.
Mrs. David Williams........................December 4th, 1883.
Joseph A. Pribyl..........................December 16th, 1883.
Mrs. Brescia Thomas......................December 17th, 1883.
William Osborn................................January 2d, 1884.
A. Hoffman Keese............................March 12th, 1884.
Mrs. Fannie Bacon ....April 27th, 1884.
Samuel Walter Nourse ....April 27th, 1884.
Moses Tobin..................................April 29th, 1884.

"Be thou faithful unto death, and I will give thee a crown of life."

"I have fought a good fight, I have finished my course. I have kept the faith."

"Him that overcometh will I make a pillar in the temple of my God, and he shall go no more out."

"The Lamb, which is in the midst of the throne, shall feed them, and shall lead them unto living fountains of waters, and God shall wipe away all tears from their eyes."

"And they shall see His face."

"He which testifieth these things, saith, Surely I come quickly.
Amen. Even so come, Lord Jesus."

> Multitude, which none can number,
> Like the stars in glory stand,
> Clothed in white apparel, holding
> Palms of victory in their hand.
>
> They have come from tribulation,
> And have washed their robes in blood,
> Washed them in the blood of Jesus;
> Tried they were, and firm they stood.
>
> Gladly, Lord, with thee they suffered,
> Gladly, Lord, with thee they died;
> And by death to life immortal,
> They were born and glorified.
>
> Now they reign in heavenly glory,
> Now they walk in golden light,
> Now they drink, as from a river,
> Holy bliss and infinite.
>
> Love and peace they taste forever,
> And all truth and knowledge see
> In the beatific vision
> Of the Blessed Trinity.

WILLIAM OSBORN.

An honored elder in the Third Church, who, in its early history, gave not only strength and time, but wealth for its prosperity, and never failed to guard its interests with a loving vigilance. He fell asleep, in a ripe old age, having nobly finished the work which his Master entrusted to his care. The session would gratefully acknowledge the debt they owe to the fidelity and zeal of this revered brother, and his name and memory will always be cherished in our church as of a sincere Christian and a pillar of spiritual strength.

"He rests from his labors, and his works do follow him."

"*Faithful unto death.*"

JOHN S. CARPENTER — CHAS. F. CHESSMAN.

The session would place upon its records their deep sorrow in the unexpected deaths of two of its most honored members of the Church and most reliable officers, Bros. John S. Carpenter and Chas. F. Chessman. Though these brethren had been connected with the eldership only a few years, they had become, through their earnest piety and loving unselfish devotion to the interests of the Church, strong pillars in the service of the Master, and, in our poor judgment, they could not be spared from the field where they so joyfully labored; but we bow in submission to His will "who doeth all things well," assured that "our loss is their eternal gain."

MEMBERS RECEIVED

FROM MAY, 1883, TO MAY, 1884.

On Confession of Christ 101
By letter from other churches............................. 112

    Total for year 213

Dismissed by letter.. 99
Total membership...2,183

NAMES OF MEMBERS

UNITING WITH THE CHURCH FROM MAY, 1883, TO MAY, 1884.

Albert, Mrs. Frances.
Alden, Mrs. Frances M.
Allen, Alex. M.
Armstrong, James.
Austin, Miss Hattie M.
Averill, Miss Carrie.

Baker, Everett S.
Baldwin, Mrs. Charlotte.
Beach, Edward P.
Beach, Mrs. Julia E.
Beers, Miss Bessie.
Blaikie, Miss Elizabeth A.
Bobo, Mrs. Ella F.
Briggs, Theophilus.
Briggs, Mrs. Mary E.
Brown, Miss Elizabeth.
Brown, Miss Isabella.
Brown, Miss Jennie.
Bruton, James J.
Bulkley, Robert H.
Bulkley, Mrs. Margaret F.

Cantner, Mrs. Frank C.
Capner, Mrs. Margaret B.
Carner, Miss Julia F.
Caution, David.
Caution, Mrs. Ellen B.
Chase, Murray C.
Chrystal, Wm. L.
Cleveland, Miss Laura B.
Cobb, Mrs. Augusta D.
Cook, Ezekiel H.

Cook, Mrs. Clara.
Cox, Chas. W.
Craik, Mrs. Grace L.

Davis, Mrs. Mary A.
Davis, Miss Mary L.
Doerr, Edward F.
Downs, Mrs. Sarah A.
Drake, James.
Drake, Mrs. Isabella.
Drummond, Mrs. Catherine E.
Duff, Edward H.

Ealy, Elijah R.
Ealy, Mrs. Nettie.
Edwards, Sherman T.
Edwards, Miss Maggie A.
Elliott, Mrs. Mary E.
Elliott, Robert J.
Elliott, Miss Ada W.
Elliott, Miss Edith.
Evans, Mrs. Harriet E.
Ewing, Wm. B.
Ewing, Mrs. Lucy H.

Fish, Chas. E.
Fisher, John.
Foxley, Miss Clara A.

Galpin, Richard H.
Gardiner, Mrs. Charlotte.
Garrott, Miss Florence Lee.
Gates, Frank A.

THIRD PRESBYTERIAN CHURCH.

George, Miss Elizabeth.
Gillespie, John.
Gillespie, Mrs. Keturah.
Gillespie, Chas. E.
Gillespie, Miss Hattie M.
Gordon, Daniel C.
Gordon, Mrs.
Graham, Jas. J.
Graham, Wm.
Griswold, James.

Hansens, Bewnie.
Harlan, Mrs. Eliza J.
Harlan, Miss Rosalie M.
Harlan, Miss Bessie M.
Haynes, Fred'k T.
Hebard, Jas. L.
Henderson, Miss Ada T.
Hoge, A. H.
Hoge, Mrs. Jane C.
Hoglen, Mrs. R. S.
Holden, Walter S.
Holden, Nelson B.
Holden, Mrs. Katie S.
Howard, Joseph J.
Howard, Mrs. Mary.
Howland, Miss Amelia.
Hunter, Miss Harriet J.
Hurd, Robt. A.
Hutchinson, Miss Mabel C.

Jewell, Ira H.
Jones, Fred'k H.
Jones, Mrs. Elizabeth D.
Johnson, Olaf A.
Johnson, Miss Josephine A.

Kammerer, Wm. S.
Kammerer, Mrs. Mattie G.
Keehn, Geo. W.

Ker, Miss Mary.
Ker, Miss Sarah V.
Kerr, Miss Annie E.
Kidder, Miss Frances M. A.
Kittredge, Mrs. Jane B.
Kittredge, George A.

Latshaw, Mrs. Texie F.
Lay, Robt. H.
Lay, Mrs. Sarah J.
Lay, Miss Georgiella.
Le Vally, Mrs. Lettie.
Lockwood, Sam'l T.
Lockwood, Mrs. Juliette P.
Lockwood, Sam'l P.
Lockwood, Miss Edna May.
Long, Mrs. Jane S.
Lundgren, Sven A.
Lundgren, Mrs. Matilda A.

Mac Kay, Mrs. Jessie.
Mc Callum, Wm.
Mc Cormick, Chas. A.
Mc Cormick, Mrs. Amy S.
Mc Creight, Samuel L.
Mc Cullough, Wm. H.
Mc Henry, Daniel.
Mc Murry, John.
Miller, Miss Alice.
Miller, Mrs. Esther P.
Mills, Mrs. Mary F.
Mitchell, Archibald.
Mowen, Simeon J.
Mowen, Mrs. Laura E.
Mullin, Mrs. Annie.
Munger, Miss Sarah M.
Murray, Alex. G.

Nichols, Mrs.
Noyes, Victor C.

THIRD PRESBYTERIAN CHURCH.

Olson, Miss Emma M.
O'Neill, Mrs. Venia.
Overbaugh, Edgar M.
Overbaugh, Mrs. Ella F.

Palmer, Mrs. Emily A.
Patterson, Mrs. Lydia A.
Patterson, Wm. R.
Patterson, Mrs. Ida L.
Paulson, Miss Mary M.
Pease, Erastus S.
Pease, Mrs. Mary L.
Petersen, John.
Petersen, Mrs. Nettie F.
Phillips, John H.
Phillips, Mrs. Florence.
Phillips, Miss Florence M.
Pitt, Mrs. Rebecca.
Pitt, Miss Lizzie H.
Pitt, Miss Alice M.
Powell, Myron H.

Ramsdell, Electus.
Ramsdell, Mrs. Carrie E.
Reid, James Mc B.
Rockey, Isaac W.
Rogers, James Gamble.

Salveson, Mrs. Susan A.
Saunders, Thos. H.
Saunders, Miss Marianne C.
Scott, Thos. L. A.
Shields, Mrs. Elizabeth G.
Shields, Miss Jennette.
Shields, Miss Emma M.
Shivers, Geo. B.
Simpson, Mrs. Mary.
Simpson, Miss Lillie M.
Smith, Mrs. Elizabeth L.
Smith, Miss Juliet C.

Smith, Mrs. Wm. B.
Smith, Miss Nellie B.
Spinning, Isaac P.
Spinning, Mrs. Rose.
Spinning, Geo. F.
Spinning, Miss Clara H.
Spooner, Miss Carrie.
Squires, Miss Carrie M.
Stagg, John L.
Stagg, Mrs. Jennie.
Stanwood, Mrs. Mary C.
Stephenson, Wm.
Swift, Fred. Thayer.

Tichenor, Mrs. Kate R.
Tiffany, Mrs. Martha.
Tomlinson, Wm. M.
Trimingham, Benjamin L.

Vaillencourt, Mrs. Harriet D.
Vaillencourt, Miss Florence A.
Vaillencourt, Miss Nellie I.
Van Steenberg, Mrs. Margaret D.

Wales, Mrs. Anna.
Walker, Chas. F.
Watson, Aquila.
Warren, James L.
Webber, Miss Louisa.
White, Alfred S.
White, Miss Jessie L.
Wickoff, Benjamin D.
Williams, Chas. S.
Wilson, Jas. J.
Wilson, Mrs. Josephine.
Wilson, Irwin D.
Wilson, Wiley H.
Wood, Thos. J.
Woodman, Miss Ella F.

Young, Robt. S.

www.ingramcontent.com/pod-product-compliance
Lightning Source LLC
Chambersburg PA
CBHW032239080426
42735CB00008B/926